I DON'T CARE
about YOUR BAND

Praise for Julie Klausner
and *I Don't Care About Your Band*

"Julie Klausner has the perfect comedic voice for a new generation of ladies—brave, self-deprecating, high-larious beyond, and brand spanking new. It's one of those books that you take to bed with you, that keeps you up all night, and that makes you laugh so hard in public the next morning that strangers ask you what you're reading. And make me so glad I'm not dating."

—Jill Soloway, author of *Tiny Ladies in Shiny Pants*
and executive producer of *United States of Tara*

"If you think dating can't get any worse, then you haven't read this book. Julie Klausner's hilarious memoir will remind you that the worse the date, the better the story it'll eventually make. If nothing else, you'll be comforted by the fact that YOUR blind date was never arrested for kidnapping."   —Em & Lo, EMandLO.com

"Julie Klausner is Helen *Girly* Brown: hard-working, yet lusty! Romantic *and* intelligent! But best of all: unapologetic about wanting to be in love. *I Don't Care About Your Band* has more wit and all of the *tsuris* of Carrie Bradshaw's *Sex and the City*, without the pithy bromides."   —Sarah Thyre, author of *Dark at the Roots*
and actress on *Strangers with Candy*

"All those misplaced orgasms and disappointing hookups with deviants were well worth it. Julie Klausner's memoir is screamingly funny and wiser than a hooker with health insurance. Take it home for a ride!"   —Michael Musto

"Klausner fashions a breathy, vernacular-veering-into-vulgar, spastically woe-filled account of her youthful heartaches falling for guys who were just not that into her."   —*Publishers Weekly*

I DON'T CARE
about YOUR BAND

WHAT I LEARNED FROM INDIE ROCKERS,
TRUST FUNDERS, PORNOGRAPHERS,
FAUX SENSITIVE HIPSTERS, FELONS,
AND OTHER GUYS I'VE DATED

Julie Klausner

GOTHAM BOOKS

PUBLISHER'S NOTE
Some names and identifying characteristics have been changed to protect the privacy of the
individuals involved.

GOTHAM BOOKS
Published by Penguin Group (USA) Inc.
375 Hudson Street, New York, New York 10014, U.S.A.
Penguin Group (Canada), 90 Eglinton Avenue East, Suite 700, Toronto, Ontario M4P 2Y3, Canada
(a division of Pearson Penguin Canada Inc.) • Penguin Books Ltd, 80 Strand, London WC2R 0RL,
England • Penguin Ireland, 25 St Stephen's Green, Dublin 2, Ireland (a division of Penguin Books
Ltd) • Penguin Group (Australia), 250 Camberwell Road, Camberwell, Victoria 3124, Australia
(a division of Pearson Australia Group Pty Ltd) • Penguin Books India Pvt Ltd, 11 Community
Centre, Panchsheel Park, New Delhi—110 017, India • Penguin Group (NZ), 67 Apollo Drive,
Rosedale, North Shore 0632, New Zealand (a division of Pearson New Zealand Ltd) • Penguin
Books (South Africa) (Pty) Ltd, 24 Sturdee Avenue, Rosebank, Johannesburg 2196, South Africa

Penguin Books Ltd, Registered Offices: 80 Strand, London WC2R 0RL, England

Published by Gotham Books, a member of Penguin Group (USA) Inc.

First printing, January 2010
10 9 8 7 6 5 4 3 2 1

Lyrics to "Fuck and Run" reprinted with permission from Liz Phair.

Gotham Books and the skyscraper logo are trademarks of Penguin Group (USA) Inc.

LIBRARY OF CONGRESS CATALOGING-IN-PUBLICATION DATA

Klausner, Julie.
    I don't care about your band : what I learned from indie rockers, trust funders, pornographers,
faux sensitive hipsters, felons, and other guys I've dated / by Julie Klausner.
        p. cm.
    ISBN 978-1-592-40561-9
    1. Dating (Social customs)—Humor. 2. Man-woman relationships—Humor. I. Title.
    PN6231.D3K57 2010
    306.7302'07—dc22   2009036016

Printed in the United States of America
Set in Bembo • Designed by Spring Hoteling

Penguin is committed to publishing works of quality and integrity.
In that spirit, we are proud to offer this book to our readers;
however, the story, the experiences, and the words
are the author's alone.

FOR MY PARENTS

I love you so much it is actually ridiculous. Thank you for your unwavering support in every single one of my creative and personal
endeavors and beyond. Next time, I promise I'll write a book you
can read.

contents

Introduction   ix

SECTION ONE: HERE COMES MY CHILDHOOD!

Broadway, Daddy, and Other Barriers to Loving Me   3

Kermit the Frog Is a Terrible Boyfriend   13

Never Tell Them What You're Actually Wearing   21

Be Your Own Gay Best Friend   33

Twin Cities   45

SECTION TWO: . . . AND OTHER ATROCITIES

The Rules   59

Power of Three   67

CONTENTS

White Noise   75

Turn Down the Glamour   85

Star Wars Is a Kids' Movie   95

SECTION THREE: "CRAZY" IS AN STD

Sweet Sweeney Agonistes   111

The Critic   123

Douche Ziggy   141

Giants and Monsters   161

SECTION FOUR: EXILE IN GUYVILLE

Paper Clips Versus Larry Flynt   175

I Don't Care About Your Band   189

So You Want to Date a Musician   203

The Kid   209

Did I Come to Brooklyn for This?   221

Red Coats and Mary Wilkies   231

SECTION FIVE: THE HOUSE OF NO

Old Acquaintances   243

Acknowledgments   253

About the Author   257

introduction

Two things about me before we get started.

First of all, I will always be a subscriber to the sketch comedy philosophy of how a scene should unfold, which is "What? That sounds crazy! OK, I'll do it."

The other thing is, I love men like it is my job.

I LOVE men so much that I've never once considered what it would be like to "take a break" from dating them, or to focus my mind on other things besides falling in love with one, or to look for work in a field that's more female-dominated, or anything else lesbians suggest you do after a guy breaks your heart. And despite repetitive instances of heartbreak, humiliations, failures, and mistakes I've accumulated, I've never stopped casting myself as the straight man in the sketch who agrees to do something bonkers; who submits to the recklessness and absurdity of optimism, time and time again.

Here is why: I could never give up on the possibility of falling for someone who'd make all of the pies I took in the face worthwhile. And this is a book about how frustrating it is to keep returning to something disappointing you will not give up on.

I am, by nature, an expert grudge hoarder. But I don't save up my grudges for breakups—for me, it's the disappointments that haunt me like Fail Ghosts. I dwell and retread and mourn relationships that could have been with characters you'll meet soon. There are some doozies! And I haven't even included the story about the guy I met at a Korean barbecue restaurant who said, after I remarked on the grill built into our table, that the place was perfect for a blind date, because, "if you don't like your date's face, you can just mash it into the grill." That guy deserves a book of his own, but I think Bret Easton Ellis already wrote it.

What follows in this book are selective stories of guys who came on strong, then sputtered out; high hopes shattered by mucky realities; and romantic miscarriages I had to clean up myself, which is as gross as it sounds.

I DID not embark on the task of writing this book for the sake of basking in my own woe, *Cathy* cartoonlike. And by no means is this a cathartic assemblage of "He Done Me Wrong" stories served hot. I'm not PJ Harvey, and this isn't 1998. I wrote these stories strewn with romantic collateral damage because I think they're funny now that I've stopped crying, and because I learned things from them I hope will resonate with women who've snacked on similarly empty fare when it comes to guys.

And there are so many *guys*. I remember the first time a friend referred to a guy I liked as a "man," and I made a face like I was asking Willis what he was talkin' 'bout. A man is hard to find, good or otherwise, but guys are everywhere now. That's why women go nuts for Don Draper on *Mad Men*. If that show was called *Mad Guys,* it might star Joe Pesci, and nobody wants to see that.

Meanwhile, I know way more women than girls. There's a whole generation of us who rode on the wings of feminism's entitlement like it was a Pegasus with cornrows, knowing how smart we were and how we could be anything. The problem is that we ended up at the mercy of a generation of guys who don't quite seem to know what's expected of them, whether it's earning a double income or texting someone after she blows you. There are no more traditions or standards, and manners are like cleft chins or curly hair—they only run in some families.

It seems like everybody is just confused.

I know grown women who flip out like teenyboppers once they sense a sea change in a guy who seemed to be in it for the long haul but got scared after some innocuous exchange, and now they feel responsible. ("I shouldn't have sent that text with that dumb joke!") There are ladies who hook up instead of date because those are the crumbs to feast on when they are starving. Women who feel awful because they knew a guy was bad news, but got involved anyway, then got attached, and now they feel terrible not just because biology kicked in—"I had an orgasm and I like him now!"—but because they *feel bad for feeling bad*. Like it wasn't enough just to feel bad because he didn't call you after his dick was inside you. Now, you have to feel bad because you're not *allowed* to feel bad.

Because we can hook up just to hook up now. Because you

knew what you were getting into. And you did anyway. But then everything changed.

And instead of being the way some guys are at that age, let's say in their late thirties, and they've never been married, and there's a ticking clock but they don't hear it because they're like, "My career!" or "Look at all these twenty-five-year-old girls who let me make out with them even though they didn't when I was in high school!"—you *don't* shut yourself off. You don't stop trying to connect. You don't close up like a clam, even when it gets hard to tell the difference between who you are and how you are treated.

You keep trying, in the nature of optimism; in the nature of *believing in humanity*, like Carole King told our moms to do. And when you cry about things not working out, you're crying not only because a guy you slept with now doesn't seem to care you're alive for some reason that's beyond everything you've been told by teachers, parents, friends and everybody else who knows how awesome you are—who helped make you that way—but also, because you're ashamed of yourself for crying.

IT'S PART of the female disposition to take the blame for failed things. We're not as entitled as men, even fictional ones, like Will Hunting, who only needed Robin Williams to scream "It's not your fault!" to board the self-esteem bus after breaking down. Meanwhile, when we get hurt, we're ashamed right away.

You stop confiding in people when they ask why you're upset, because you don't want to enter a debate on a side you can't defend. You feel like you were wrong taking a chance on a guy you should've known couldn't give you what you wanted, and in a way, you feel you deserved what you got.

But here's the thing: You sanction that kind of behavior

when you keep quiet. When you don't tell your friends it happened because you're ashamed of what you did and how you reacted to it, and you rationalize that it was something you did that made him shy away. That it was because you slept with him too soon. Because you didn't play hard to get. You didn't follow the rules and you failed to act like a hooker who just shrugs and moves on to the next conquest, like those are the only two things a girl can do.

You blame your own fundamental attractiveness, figuring that somewhere in between him pursuing you and his losing interest, you did something that made him stop liking you. You called him too soon or too much. You made a dumb joke. You texted him too late after he texted you, and then he didn't respond. Maybe he hated your taste in the books he saw on your shelf. Maybe he cringed when you used that emoticon in your last e-mail. Or maybe somehow, he caught wind of your secret—that you were actually unlovable. Needy, ugly, fat, desperate, whatever it is you're afraid of guys finding out you are or you think you are—even if it's a person who just has the balls to remain ardently committed to the act of falling in love.

So you tell yourself that you're practicing the art of connecting and disconnecting, in hopes that the latter will get easier the more it happens. That you'll get more casual with practice. But you don't.

And you feel worse each time. And you figure it's because you're a big, dumb idiot for wanting to keep taking chances.

Well, guess what? You're pretty smart for an idiot. And I wrote this book for you and everybody else after my own sloppy, panting heart who, despite our disappointments, trudge on, looking for what we know is real.

It's just got to be.

SECTiON ONE

here comes my childhood!

"Sex is the great leveler, taste the great divider."

—Pauline Kael, *For Keeps*

"You *are* special! *Never* stop believing that!"

—Daddy Warbucks, in *Annie*

broadway, daddy, and other barriers to loving me

There are two kinds of girls who drift toward the more unsavory characters in the dating pool. There are, first of all, the kind of girls who've been ignored, abandoned, or otherwise treated ambivalently by their dads, and look to creeps as a means of replicating the treatment to which they've grown accustomed. These are the kind of girls who endure neglect, hostility, rigorous mind-fuckings, repetitive late-night texts that start "Hey, I'm in your neighborhood . . ." or long stretches of total disappearance from men who reinforce their earliest-learned notion of how a boy should treat a girl. Some of them strip. Some of them strip ironically. Plenty are a great deal of fun at dinner parties.

The other kind of girls who wallow in the Valley of the Dipsticks are the ones who know they deserve better. These are the girls with the great dads; the ones who had their decks stacked from the outset, who knew it couldn't get any better in the guy department than the one who taught her how to ride her bike. This is the princess who knows only to la-la-la-la-la-la-live for today, confident she will always have her daddy to lavish her with the spoils of high-octane attention once the bastard of the week flies the turkey coop. She already has a mensch on the back burner, so in the suitor department, she is not looking for much of a multitasker—just like the married man who doesn't care whether his mistress can get along with his friends. This category of girls, in which I include myself, has a tendency to exceed her allotted bullshit quota for boys she likes, if only because her stubborn mind will not reconcile the notion of wonderful things ever coming to an end.

My dad was the first man I ever loved so much it hurt. He was always around, from our current-events chat over bowls of Total in the morning, to the most catastrophic of devastations, like when I was ten, and something I thought was horrible happened to me. I hadn't made it past the second callback for a community theater production of *Annie*.

I mourned my soiled future as my father and I sped home along the Sprain Parkway in the family Toyota Cressida. We were twenty minutes past the exit for Briarcliff Manor when I finally stopped sobbing. My dad, trying to seem sympathetic, told me to listen to the radio; that it would help distract me. I stared out the window, watching my dreams die.

My ten-year-old mind had figured that starring as Annie in a production of the show of the same name would have finally provided me with sweet, elusive, abstract victory. I knew I could play that role better than any of my peers from camp and school. But this production—the one I didn't get—was going to be cast with *actual adults* in the roles of the grown-up characters in the show; adults like Oliver Warbucks, the billionaire, and Lily St. Regis, the squeaky-voiced trollop. And that made the rejection even worse.

Like a lot of nerdy kids, I was a bit too congenial with grown-ups. I competed for the attention of teachers and my parents' friends like they were the ones who could rescue me from the company of kids my age, and usher me, via minivan, into the promised land of Eileen Fisher tunics and Merlot. I wanted so badly, in general, to be in the company of elders. And this play—not just any play, but *Annie*, the quintessential '80s musical about narcissism and striving—seemed like a perfect chance to work in tandem with adults. The kind of people who have checking accounts and pubic hair! I ached with singular ambition to hold hands with an actual grown-up man with a shorn head or in a bald cap, and croon in counterpoint, *"I'm poor as a mouse!" "I'm richer than Midas!"* musically articulating the main way in which Annie and Oliver Warbucks were different.

Sundry dumb fantasies about being onstage suchly pranced about my noggin with cartoonish frequency around that time, fueling my case for a long car ride up to Yorktown, which I laid out point by point in efforts to convince my parents to haul me upstate to the audition. They did, and while I speed-belted the first two bars of "Tomorrow" in a lineup of five other third-graders, my mother made small talk with the other kids' stage mothers. My mom was always encouraging, but she was no Mama Rose: The idea of time wasted at commercial auditions or tuition thrown at acting schools that gave out homework assignments like "go to the zoo and observe an animal" was dismissible by her as something done for kids who aren't terribly bright.

I, thrillingly, made the cut at round one of the tryouts,

so in between that first night and three days later, when my dad drove me to my callback, I'd already counted, battered, and deep-fried all possible chickens. I'd written my bio for the program, which made generous employ of the phrases "auburn songstress" and "unwavering gratitude," told off my enemies in my hypothetical Tony Award acceptance speech ("Who's a fat retard *now*?"), and practiced signing autographs in a stage name I'd chosen—"Kitty Clay"—that was better suited to a 1950s character actress who only played prostitutes. I had set myself up for a mighty descent.

My father, atonally humming along to "Up On the Roof" on 101.1 CBS-FM, was privately happy I hadn't made the cut. Not because he didn't encourage my performative instincts: in fact, "supportive" was a tepid modifier for the kind of pride my father took in watching me onstage. He loved watching me captivate and made sure I knew I was star-stuff, and was always front row center at all of my school performances, ready with flowers and praise, even after the doozies. Like when the accompanist at the Y disclosed, at the last minute, that she did not have the sheet music to *Gypsy*, and I opted over "a cappella" and "not at all" to give a fully-committed performance of "Rose's Turn" along to a cassette of the score from the production starring Tyne Daly, complete with Claudia Teitelbaum providing the off-stage "Yeah!" in between "You like it?" and "Well, I got it," which, from an eight-year-old girl, is technically performance art.

No, my dad was just relieved that I didn't get the part because now he was off the hook in the chauffeur department. It was an hour-and-a-half commute back and forth from Scarsdale to Yorktown Heights, where rehearsals were held, and if I'd been cast as Annie, or even one of her ragtag orphan chums—a demotive possibility that hadn't even darkened the doorway of my ego-addled young mind—he would have had to drive me back and forth five days a week or risk breaking my heart by telling me no. And the sound of that word was always jarring coming from his lips, whether it referenced a third cookie or the actualization of a grandiose fantasy. My mother told me weeks later, once I'd calmed down, that they wouldn't have driven me to rehearsals if I'd made it, but took the "We'll cross that bridge!" attitude when she first took me to the audition. My mom, ever-presumptive of her conversation partner's familiarity with the idiomatic canon, never finished the second part of clichés. From her, it was always "A stitch in time" or "The apple doesn't fall," which was deeply confusing advice to a little girl merely trying to make sense of why Andrea Blum—a popular classmate whose mother was a backstabbing monster with an eye-lift that made her look Korean—stole my Doritos.

Being in that play, I reasoned, would have emancipated me from the social oppression I heroically endured daily at the French-manicured hands of the Alpha Jewesses of Solomon Schecter Hebrew School. I was so tired of being at the business end of the sneer of Andrea Blum, not to mention Lizzies Shapiro, Steinberg, and Strauss—the tannest girls with the longest lashes and the scratchiest Benetton sweaters in the grade, whose precocious sarcasm was rivaled only by alpha girls with blossoming breast buds in junior high. I wanted so badly to get this role and bid "Later, losers!" to them all. They'd see me from the cheap seats, I thought. And I'd be onstage with a grown man and a live dog. The sobbing recommenced.

My dad, now feebly whistling along to "Under the Board-walk," told me to relax. It was good advice with a beginning, middle, and an end that I couldn't heed, hysterical in the wake of my rejection. What kind of terrible mistake had been made? I thought I had the lead in the bag when I arrived at the open call and saw I was the only redhead auditioning. Everybody knows Annie has red hair, and who wants to put a wig on a kid without leukemia? I was prepared, too, having practiced along to both the movie and the album from the Broadway show, tapping on carpet in my bedroom and letting, respectively, Albert Finney and Reid Shelton promise Annie/me that he didn't need sunshine to turn his skies to blue, *"I don't need anything but you!"*

In reality, a little girl needs more than her dad, even if he is Oliver Warbucks, the moneyed plutocrat with the heart defrostable only by the Depression-era optimism of a carrot-topped hobo. But my father, who instilled in me a love of musical theater so potent that I am unable to listen to the cast recording of *Sunday in the Park with George* without bursting into tears, gave me the impression when I was growing up that he was the only man I'd ever need.

My father is a stocky accountant of modest height with a Bronx accent and a bald spot who smiles with his eyes. He is amused by stories as simple as "I saw a golden retriever with a toy in his mouth walking down the street today." He is an impossibly warm man: When he shakes your hand, he's probably touching your shoulder as well, and he always looks at me after he cracks a joke at the dinner table, to make sure I know he was goofing for my benefit. He always kept an eye on me, making sure I called home if I was spending the night at a friend's house or going into the city, and whenever I protested at his protective overtures, he'd just say, "You're my only daughter," which I took to mean that I was the only person in the world.

My dad is used to acting the part of patriarch since his

father—the one I'm named after—died from a heart attack at a young age. The middle child of three boys, and, from what I glean, a bit of a rumpus-starter in his adolescence, one of the chief defining characteristics of my father is, perhaps idiosyncratically, his deep appreciation of musicals. He still talks about the first Broadway show he ever saw: *Li'l Abner,* a show that is, like *Annie,* based on an ancient, ridiculous comic strip. He recalls sitting starry-eyed as a youngster in an orchestra seat as actors bleated the show-stopping "Jubilation T. Cornpone" number, agape at the spectacle of it all. But although he always loved musical theater, my father was never a performer. Even if he had the ability to carry a tune in a steel-lined bucket, it's not his nature to take the spotlight. He's the guy who shines it.

It's an untrue stereotype to say all gay guys love musicals, but it's a pretty good ballpark generalization to say there aren't a ton of straight men under fifty who thrill when told the planned activity for the evening starts with a cab ride up to Times Square and ends when Tommy Tune takes a bow. Heterosexual men typically abhor the pageantry of musical theater; its broad humor, the artifice of a character breaking out into a full-throat ballad during a tender moment, the camp of it all, at once terribly out of date and in questionable taste. What I personally delight in—the humor inherent to stuff so bad it's good, or at least funny—is a language unintelligible to many a girl-liking boy, with the exception of certain types of straights like tea-sipping PBS-aficionados and actors, who are gay by definition, because all actors are in love with themselves.

It was at the age of eleven or so, soon after I lost that role in *Annie,* when I realized that my ability to sing, dance, and generally captivate an audience including but not limited to my father in the front row was not a guaranteed means of seducing dudes. Twenty years later, once I'd abandoned musical theater to be a comedy writer, I would learn that being funny wasn't either.

I WAS at sleep-away camp, playing Rusty Charlie in boy drag in *Guys & Dolls*, when I sang the bafflingly titled "Fugue for Tinhorns" number, bedecked in an oil-paint mustache, a man's tweed jacket, and a French braid that a counselor tucked beneath a plastic derby hat. It was as though I was the recipient of some perverse challenge that dared me to feel pretty. But at the time, I was wholly confident that my performance, mustachioed or not, would close the deal with the boy whom I'd, until then, had only flirted with at socials. His name was Evan Pringsheim, and he hailed from exotic Chappaqua. We were paired off once I told my bunk I liked his face, a gossip morsel my campmates broadcasted to Evan's friends, who chanted, "Do it!" until he was literally pushed, red-faced, from of a lineup of his contemporaries, into my general direction, like a cannibal tribe's offering of a virgin into a volcano's simmering maw. I was delighted. Mine, all mine!

I'd pulled out all the stops with Evan during our five-p.m. encounters, telling him jokes I'd stolen from the "Truly Tasteless" collections I'd browsed at B. Dalton and about the time I lost that tooth. All the while, I was clad in my fail-safe boy bait outfit: the neon pink T-shirt that bellowed LA JOLLA, CALIFORNIA in banana yellow all-caps, and my "fancy shorts." It was a lethal combination—a veritable bustier-back/seamed stockings combo—but Evan hadn't kissed me yet. I knew that once he saw me work that round in "Fugue"—the one where all of the gangsters are singing over each other about the horses they think are best to wager on—he would belong to me.

So, I was wrong. Wrong like Hitler was wrong. But for a couple of hours that night, while I was blissfully distracted onstage at sleep-away camp, I missed my father less. Evan didn't say anything after the show: I think he was being kind, in a way, pretending it never happened. Like he didn't have to sit there and watch his girlfriend in mustache makeup singing, *"Just a minute, boys! I've got the feed box noise! It says the great-grandfather was Equipoise."* Maybe he figured out that he if pretended it never happened, one day he'd be able to get an erection.

Evan had alchemized something embarrassing into something invisible, and his nonreaction to my pursuit marked the first of a lifelong trend. As long as I can remember, I've had to fight off urges to chase and conquer boys who seem blasé. It's decidedly unladylike.

Men who disclose obsessions with girls from day one are Don Juan or Alexander Portnoy. But I am amorous the way fat people are hungry. When I have a crush on someone, I feel like Divine in *Hairspray*, warning everyone in her proximity that her diet pill is wearing off. My enduring pursuit of the opiates provided only from male attention, glorious male attention, has destined me to a lifetime of displays of unseemly and comically humiliating behavior.

EVAN PRINGSHEIM of Chappaqua was the first of many would-be beaus unable to circumnavigate the wall of Daddy I'd erected on all sides of me, its bricks held together by the mortar of song and dance. When Evan dumped me at the end of the summer, I wailed like I did in my dad's car, taking refuge back home in the comfort of my parents and my brother, who told me, after what was ostensibly my first breakup, that "Men are slime."

I took to heart that christening philosophy, but it didn't make me feel any better after I'd been let down. I've just always wanted a boyfriend, OK? Just like I wanted Cookie Crisp on my birthday and that Barbie named Miko who was supposed to be Hawaiian and came with her own tie-dyed bathing suit.

But boys and roles aren't things you can tear from shelves and take to the cash register. You have to put yourself out there, sing your eight bars, and then wait to hear if you're the one who makes sense for the gig. And if it doesn't work out? Well, then you've got to make sure that somebody who loves you is around to remind you there will always be another show.

kermit the frog
is a terrible boyfriend

When *The Muppet Movie* aired on network TV in the early 1980s, my family used the VHS tape that came with our first-generation General Electric brand VCR to record it. I wore that cassette down to its black plastic casing, repeatedly delighting in the travails of Kermit and his friends on the lam from frog-leg baron Doc Hopper, and grooving right along to the Electric Mayhem. I was in preternatural awe of the character actresses in the film: Madeline Kahn, Carol Kane, and Cloris Leachman all had cameos, and I still credit that movie for my Austin Pendleton crush. But more than anything, as a little girl, I wanted to be exactly like Miss Piggy. She was *ma héroïne*.

I was a plucky little girl, but I never related to the rough-and-tumble icons of children's lit, like Pippi Longstocking or Harriet the Spy. Even Ramona Quimby, who seemed cool, wasn't somebody I could super-relate to. She was scrawny and scrappy, and I was soft and sarcastic. I connected instead to Miss—never "Ms."—Piggy; the comedienne extraordinaire who'd alternate eyelash bats with karate chops, swoon over girly stuff like chocolate, perfume, feather boas or random words pronounced in French, then, on a dime, lower her voice to "Don't fuck with me, fellas" decibel when slighted. She was hugely feminine, boldly ambitious, and hilariously violent when she didn't get her way, whether it was in work, love, or life. And even though she was a pig puppet voiced by a man with a hand up her ass, she was the fiercest feminist I'd ever seen.

I took my cues from Piggy, chasing every would-be Kermit in my vicinity with porcine voracity and what I thought was feminine charm. I was aggressive. I never went through a "boys are gross" phase—I'd find a crush and press my hoof to the gas pedal. I wasn't the girl who couldn't say no—I was the one who wouldn't hear it. I left valentines on the desk of my first-grade crush, Jake Zucker, weeks into March. I cornered Avi Kaplan in the hallway and tried to make him kiss me. I begged my mom to tell Ben Margulies's mom about my crush on him in second grade, in hopes she'd put in a good word for me, like that has ever worked.

I didn't think of myself then as I do now, in retrospect; as a pigtailed, red-faced mini-Gulliver, clomping around in Keds and a loud sweater, my thunder thighs tucked into stonewash casing. I'd catch the scent of "a *MAAAAAAAN!*" and want to club a cute boy I liked on the head and drag him by the hair to a cave, where I could force him to like me back. But at the time, I thought of myself as a *pig fatale*. Miss Piggy wanted what I did, which was to be famous and fabulous and to be loved by her one true frog and occasionally Charles Grodin. But look-ing back, I realize Kermit was, for lack of a better term, just not that into her.

So much about Kermit the Frog is intrinsically lovable: his sense of humor, his loyalty to his friends, his charm and confidence in who he is, despite the challenges of being green. But at the same time, Kermit has a distinct indifference to the overtures of his would-be paramour that I came to expect from the boys who crossed my path from grade school on. I think watching Piggy chase Kermit gave me an odd sense of what men and women do, in real life, when they're adults. I figured that if you—glamorous, hilarious, fabulous you—find a boy who's funny and popular and charming and shy, and you want him, you just go out and "Hi-Ya" yourself into his favor. Piggy and Kermit represented the quintessential romance to me. And I don't know how healthy that was.

Watching *The Muppet Movie* again recently gave me a feel-ing of déjà vu, and not in the way you expect when you watch a movie you loved as a kid. As I watched Kermit haplessly bik-ing down the street without a care in the world, about to be smushed between two steamrollers, I thought, "Oh my God. I know that guy. I've dated him." Kermit, beloved frog of yore, suddenly, overwhelmingly, reminded my adult self of vintage-eyeglass-frame-wearing guys from Greenpoint or Silver Lake, who pedal along avenues in between band practice and drinks with friends, sans attachment, oblivious to the impeding haz-ards of reality and adulthood. *"Oh my God,"* I thought. Kermit is one of those hipsters who seem like they're afraid of me.

It all came together.

Remember how content Kermit was, just strumming his banjo on a tree trunk in the swamp? That's the guy I've chased my whole life, killing myself trying to show him how fabulous I am. Remember how, on *The Muppet Show*, Kermit used to politely laugh at Miss Piggy's earnest pleas for some kissy-kissy, or fend off her jealousy after flirting right in front of her with one of his pretty guest stars? Piggy had to canvas relentlessly to get herself a good part on that show, while Kermit was always the star. Because she loved him, Piggy would always take whatever he felt like giving her. And it was never anything too fancy, like the jewels she'd buy for herself. Pearls before Swine? More like bros before hos.

Kermit never appreciated what he had in Piggy, because she was just one great thing about his awesome life. He had the attitude women's magazines try to sell to their audience: that significant others are only the frosting on the cake of life. But everybody knows that cake without frosting is just a muffin.

Kermit didn't want to devote his life to making Piggy happy—he just wanted to host his show and enjoy hanging out with his friends. Anything more she'd ask of him would warrant a gulp. Do you remember *The Muppets Take Manhattan*? At the end, Piggy actually tricks Kermit into marrying her, subbing in a real minister for Gonzo in the Broadway show that calls for Kermit and Piggy's characters to get fake-married. This shit goes down after Kermit tears Piggy to pieces in front of all their friends, deriding her about how no frog like him would ever go out with a pig like her.

He gets karate-chopped, natch, and if you want to be technical about it, he wasn't Kermit then because he'd lost his memory, but this was after he'd made Piggy suffer throughout that whole film. Our poor porcine heroine had to watch her beloved carry on with a mousy human waitress (the one whose coworkers were actual mice) while she stalked him in the bushes. And she knew the whole time that Kermit's priorities lay with making good on a promise he made to his friends that they'd succeed with their show over making anything work with her.

Even after they're married, Kermit cheats Piggy out of their swan song. The two hold hands, freshly wed, and right before the movie fades out on the two of them riding a crescent moon, Kermit musters the most romantic sentiment he could possibly come up with to sing to his wife:

"What better way could anything end? Hand in hand with a friend."

His *friend*? What the ass???

I remember thinking that line was the sweetest thing ever when I watched it as a kid, and now I'm just horrified. I don't mean to forsake the romantic notion of a spouse being one's best friend, because obviously that's tear-jerking, nor to undermine the natural comedy of a frisky woman chasing a timid man—obviously that's funny, and it always has been, from Looney Tunes to Joan Rivers's perennial stand-up act about being unfuckable. But as children's entertainment, the Muppets were a parable to me. Those movies weren't Fractured Fairy Tales: they were the originals. And I think, just as I strove to emulate Piggy—resplendent in feather boas, lavender mules, and rings over opera gloves—I wonder how many guys from my generation looked to Kermit as an example of the coolest guy in the room.

How maybe they think it's OK to defer the advances of the fabulous woman they know is going to be there no matter what, while they dreamily pursue creative endeavors and dabble with other contenders. How maybe they learned the value of bromance from Kermit's constant emphasis on his obligations to his friends before his ball and chain. And how maybe they figured out that if you're soft-spoken and shy, but you know how to play a musical instrument, girls will come in droves. That you don't have to learn how to approach a woman or worry that she'll do anything but fly into a jealous snit if you talk to other girls in front of her. You just keep your creativity flowing and your guy friends close, and you'll have to beat the ladies down with a stick.

Sometimes I suspect Kermithood may be the model of modern masculinity. If it is, it doesn't match the matehood expectations of a generation of Miss Piggys who, at least eventually, want more. After all, since we were little, we were taught that the only point of chasing frogs is the hope that they turn into men when you kiss them.

Maybe Piggy would have been better off with Fozzie. Gonzo was a pervert and Rolf, another musician, would have been beholden to the demands of the road. And sure, stand-ups have their own problems, but I'll bet the bear at least could've made her laugh. And Piggy probably could've stood a chance to feel a bit dainty next to him, too, Fozzie being fuzzy and barrel-chested and all. There's nothing like a spindly-legged, amphibious boy who weighs less than you do to make you feel like a real hog.

Piggy's self-esteem didn't seem to ruffle from rejection after rejection, but that bitch is like Beyoncé, who is made of steel, and possibly from outer space. But when I look back and I think about chasing Jake Zucker back and forth on ice skates at his birthday party, or praying that Ben Margulies got my signed note informing him that he had a "secret" admirer, I wished I'd given myself a gentle nudge in the direction of more self-preserving endeavors. Like maybe how, if you want to be the star of a show, you should make your own effing show. Or that you need to walk away from a guy who doesn't care that you're jealous when he flirts with other people in front of you. Or maybe you'll just find out one day that instead of a popular charmer with a talent for playing the banjo, what you really want is a guy who digs you like crazy; who makes *you* feel like the star.

never tell them what you're actually wearing

There are three experiences I had in junior high that wildly influenced my nascent sexuality, and all can be traced back to Melissa Ackerman.

Melissa Ackerman was the alpha girl of a mini-clique with liberal enough standards to admit me into its ranks at age twelve. I was elated to be in the social servitude of such a horrible person.

Melissa was a mini-sociopath, according to my mom, who was getting her PhD in psychology at the time and practiced her diagnostic skills on my new friends. And indeed there was something Dexter-esque about Melissa, that jerk. She'd constantly pull Queen Bee shit on me to mess with my status. One day she'd be my best friend, the next week she'd glare at me in the cafeteria, whispering nasty things about my parakeet to her posse.

But for one glorious stretch of time, I was one of Melissa's Yes Girls, and one Saturday night, she invited me to sleep over at her house, which would turn out to be the site of Nascent Sexual Awakening Experience Number One. Also in attendance was Melissa's BFF, Hannah Ginsberg, a girl with a gummy smile and shaggy layer cut with a constantly yarmulke-wearing, bearded father; Deborah Kaiser, the basset-hound facsimile attracted to topsiders, Sally Jessy Raphael glasses frames, and probably, one day, other women; and finally, sweet relief incarnate, Ronit Yellen, the new girl from Israel by way of Massachusetts, whom I'd circled and poached, hawklike, upon catching the scent of "New person who hasn't known me since kindergarten when I was assigned my rank on the day-school pecking order and so might one day think I was awesome." We all got together at Melissa's house to watch *Dream a Little Dream*, a teen comedy intended to whimsically dampen the Hanes Her Ways of girls in our preteen demographic, starring Coreys Haim and Feldman. We were to have a girltastic time.

Melissa was spoiled by her parents, a mouthy Egyptian mom and a dad who was never around. Her bedroom was bedecked with all the trappings of a tween dream: she had a princess phone, a tiny pink TV/VCR combo, boys on the walls ripped from the pages of *Tiger Beat*, and a daybed with a trundle underneath it for Hannah, her Number Two. After Kosher pizza, Melissa led us through what she decided was sleepover-y fun. We played M.A.S.H. and found out whether we'd live in Mansions, Apartments, Shacks, or Houses when we got older. We made those origami fortune-teller things you put on your fingers so we could find out whether our husbands would be Eytan, Josh, Ben, or Yehuda after jotting down the Hebraic names of our comelier male classmates on the insides of the paper folds. We made a big deal about taking our new bras off in time for bed. And all the while, a syndicated episode of *Night Court* was on in the background that would burn an indelible impression onto my budding sexuality.

It was the episode in which John Larroquette's smarmy lawyer character, Dan Fielding, saves the life of Markie Post's goody-two-shoes character, Christine Sullivan, by using the Heimlich maneuver on her when she chokes. Because Dan saved Christine's life, the premise went, she was obligated to sleep with him. Maybe sort of fucked-up for *Night Court*, but don't forget how many prostitutes and hobos were woven into the story line of what was otherwise a pretty genial prime-time sitcom starring a magician.

It's difficult to overemphasize how erotically compelling this episode of *Night Court* was to me. I thrilled at the notion of a silver-haired, libidinous character actor old enough to be somebody's *old* dad, coercing his co-star into taking a load of cum down the same throat he'd dislodged food from earlier in the episode! I imagined Markie Post wriggling beneath John Larroquette on the floor of the hotel room he'd secured for the occasion, sick with the cheap champagne he made her drink, prostrate with extreme weakness, forced to let him enter her and pound until he finished. At the end of the episode, when Larroquette had a change of heart about their "sex-for-choking-avoidance arrangement" and his stupid conscience kicked in, I had a case of twelve-year-old blue clit that an army of Coreys couldn't slake. I drifted off in the middle of *Dream a Little Dream*, quelled by visions of Dan Fielding grunting over my arched back, holding his calloused hands over my mouth as I whimpered "no."

I spent the better part of that year in Melissa's clique, with the sporadic banishments that come along with being friends with someone wont to hate you randomly at a moment's notice. Like a lot of junior-high girls drunk on their own company, we were very excited about our little group. We came up with a code for our teachers' names we'd use in notes we'd pass among one another. We ate lunch together every day and listened to Melissa's decrees about whether or not it was cool to like Arsenio Hall or Sinead O'Connor that week. And we were religious about alternating houses for our weekly sleep-over parties.

ONE TIME, at my house, for the occasion of Nascent Sexual Awakening Experience Number Two, Hannah Ginsberg brought over a piece of contraband she'd confided to us about earlier. She'd found a copy of *Penthouse* magazine in the mail, addressed to her father—the one who looked like a rabbi—and didn't know what to make of the offending material. She described its contents on the phone incredulously, reporting, "Apparently men like to watch women pretend to have sex with one another," and that there were "are a ton of vaginas in this magazine. And they're all shaved!" From her tone, it was like Hannah had found supplies for a pipe bomb in the mail, or a catalog addressed to her dad that contained pictures of huge baby clothes for full-grown men who can only get erections wearing diapers. She was horrified.

"I just can't imagine that my *dad* would want to look at this stuff! Maybe it was a mistake that he got it?"

Yes, Hannah. It was probably a mistake.

"Then how did they know his name and address? Do you think it was a sample free copy?"

Of course, Hannah. It was probably a free promotional issue

of *Penthouse* they sent out to everyone who donated money to B'nai B'rith International that year.

I was insistent that Hannah bring over the evidence. How were we supposed to believe her without proof? All these bald pussies and fake lesbians could have been figments of her shaggy, gummy imagination. She obediently swiped the issue and brought it to our sleepover, which must have *delighted* her father.

We pored over every page, even the ads, as kids have always done when they first find porn. Melissa led the chorus of "ewwwww'" as we confirmed Hannah's dutiful reportage. There were the bald pudendae, some with cute, trimmed stripes of pubeness on their tops, like sexy Hitler mustaches, and some with the full Paul Shaffer treatment. We beheld the Sapphic ringers, an army of them, decked out in Jane Fonda leotards over neon bike shorts, scowling their glossy, red Warrant "Cherry Pie" lips in proximity to one another's glistening genitalia. There wasn't a lot of licking, spreading, or touching going on. The photos just documented instance after instance of gesturing with long manicured fingernails towards points of interest on the other model. Nipples, vulva, tongue, buttocks. Those ladies hand-modeled each other's junk the way spokesmodels show off dinette sets. I was utterly compelled by the spectacle of it. The only other pornography I'd seen before *Penthouse* was boob-oriented—my brother's issues of *Playboy* featured nature's blondest coeds heaving their racks in between ads for luxury automobiles and interviews with Griffin Dunne. But *Penthouse* was all pussy: page after page of Virginias, shot like food photography. Labia were lit and airbrushed for maximum appetizing affect, like strawberries or ham.

I woke up early the next morning and quietly fished the

magazine out of Hannah's backpack to review the spreads I'd already memorized. I read all the stories in the *Forum* and learned five new words for "vagina," including "twat," which sounded like a sound effect from the 60s *Batman* TV show. I pored over those lesbian photos like I was trying to memorize vocab for a test. I didn't want to dive in to any of those modest muffs; I was just turned on to be closer to the mind of a straight guy with a hard-on.

Hannah took away the magazine once everybody else woke up and rolled up sleeping bags, but like any first-wave pornographic material that captures your imagination while it's still forming, *Penthouse*'s content was erotically indelible. I see bike shorts sometimes and I get excited, which is weird, because they're *bike shorts.* But the most influential section of Hannah's father's filthy pussy-magazine was the *Penthouse Forum.*

It's a cliché that girls like erotica and guys like porn, because women are more verbal and men are more visual, but the truth is that the more you leave to a woman's imagination, the less you have to bet on the likelihood that she might not like the actor who plays the mechanic in whatever's the featured clip on RedTube. Today, erotica bores me. Most of it seems to be comprised of one-adjective sentences that alternate between synonyms for genitalia. Heaving. Hungry. Moist. Rod. Slit. Glistening. Taut. Mighty. Shaft. There's Beat poetry that's more linear. But at the time, I read all that stuff. I ate it up. I loved those stories. All those "I never thought it could happen to me" chestnuts; the stewardesses, the friends' wives, the cheerleaders, the hokey endings from "then we fucked all night" to "afterward, I never saw her again." And little by little, I padded out my dirty thesaurus, which is not just an *awesome* name for a jam band, but would also prove to be a valuable resource during our next fateful sleepover at Johanna Loeb's house, the site of Nascent Sexual Awakening Experience Number Three.

JOHANNA WAS a newcomer to our clique; she was tiny—like four foot nine—and freckled, with long nails and dark, straight hair down to her elbows. She lived in Riverdale, and one night, all five of us went out to the Hard Rock Café in Manhattan for her birthday dinner before coming back to her parents' apartment for her slumber party.

Here is an example of why you should never underestimate a preteen's hunger for pornography. In the hundred or so feet between the entrance of the Hard Rock and the car door of Mr. Loeb's White Acura, Ronit and I managed to buy ourselves, from the newsstand on the corner, a magazine by the name of *Stallions*. The transaction itself couldn't have taken more than thirty seconds. We were like porn-starved ninjas, or kids at Fat Camp who manage to get Mallomars on their day pass to the orthodontist. And our six dollars did not just earn us the right to gape at photos of the rock-hard erections of at least ten free-weight and hair-gel aficionados. With *Stallions*, Ronit and I were able to provide the recreational agenda for the remainder of the evening.

Melissa shepherded us into Johanna's kitchen as soon as Mr. and Mrs. Loeb went to bed, so we could pore over our newly procured booty. Unfortunately, *Stallions* was not as fertile in the gross-out department for everyone, being as we'd cut our dentata on the vaginas of yore. There were boners, sure, but no dirty stories or staged interactions. There was only beefcake, which was not as exciting as Carvel ice-cream cake—the kind with the chocolate on the bottom, vanilla on top, and crunchies in the center—which beckoned, at least to Johanna, who seemed freaked out by her new friends' porncapades. She wanted to celebrate her birthday with a screening of *Can't Buy Me Love*; she didn't expect the horn-dog travails of the new group of gal pals she'd accidentally latched herself on to. Just before we resigned ourselves to the conclusion that *Stallions* was a bust, we found the phone sex ads in the back of the magazine.

FREE FOR WOMEN! the ads shrieked in white Arial all-caps bold on a black background. SINGLES TALK LIVE! Melissa, ever-alpha, gave the go-ahead for us to call in from Johanna's landline—the blue touchtone princess mounted to the wall above the Loebs' kitchen counter—and Ronit went first. We huddled around her and listened in, trying hard not to break up in snorts.

"Hello! And welcome to Loveline," said a recording of a voiceover actress pretending to be a slut. "You're about to be connected to one of New York's hottest singles. Just stay on the line!" The archaic technology prompted Ronit to record an introduction, and she lowered her voice an octave to that "sexy" range that, when you hear it from your friends, makes you want to barf up your Hard Rock curly fries.

"Hello, my name is Danielle," Ronit said, using the name of an unpopular girl from our grade so as to better play to her audience.

"I'm a brunette, twenty-six years old, tan skin, long legs, and huge boobs. Great skin. Not fat."

Ronit's description of "herself" sounded like a letter to Santa, asking for what she wanted more than anything. The system thanked her for recording her greeting and assured us there would be horny singles on the line momentarily, if only we'd stand by.

We stood by. Everybody was flipping out, even Johanna, who'd resignedly brought out the Carvel cake for consumption on the sidelines of what was now the main event. I was mixing the vanilla ice cream into the chocolate crunchies for Carvel soup, my favorite food, when Ronit put the decidedly nonerotic hold music on speaker, per Melissa's orders. Soon, the music stopped, and there was a canned "chime" sound.

"Great news!" intoned the slutbot. "Somebody liked your profile and wants to talk to you, live!"

There was a click. And then, there was a pause that seemed to last forever. What followed was the distinctively sheepish voice of a man who'd called a "party line" in the express hope of receiving cut-rate phone sex from a nonprofessional.

"Hello?" said the sad man.

"Hello?" said Ronit's twenty-six-year-old not-fat character.

"Hi, this is Alan."

"Hi, Alan." Ronit's "Danielle" had a baritone rasp like the business end of a barbershop quartet.

Alan wanted to know what Danielle was doing.

"I'm reading *Stallions* magazine," she actually told a stranger with a hard-on.

"Oh yeah?" challenged Alan, sotto voce, trying hard to seem sexy to a twelve-year-old. "How does looking at that magazine make you feel?"

"Pretty horny," admitted Ronit-Danielle. There was muffled snickering.

"What about you?" she continued. "What are you doing?"

"I'm stroking my cock," said the only person in the situation telling the truth.

"You fucking pervert!" screamed Melissa into the speaker phone, ruining everything. She hung up and we all laughed. I felt bad for Alan, poor guy, but hope, in retrospect, that hearing a room full of laughing twelve-year-old girls made him come harder.

Hannah went next. She decided to go with an accent for the voice of her character, Tatiana. Tatiana was of Balkan descent, based on Hannah's Boris/Natasha throatiness and habit of skipping articles in her speech.

"My name Tatiana," bleated Hannah, on the party line, to another fresh rube. "How big is your boner?"

Hysterics.

When it was my turn, I felt desperately guilty that I was pranking this man on the other end of the line. I wasn't used to talking to somebody eager to at least pretend to find me attractive, and I *loved* it. He flirted, he was friendly, he wanted to have phone sex with me, and I wanted to try out all the new vagina euphemisms I learned from the *Forum*. But the girls were in the room, pressuring me to land a zinger so we could all enjoy the folly. So, we hung up on the guy, and then, retired to our sleeping bags. And as soon as Ronit's snoring filled the dark room like the scent of a pumpkin candle, I, once more, Grinch-like, silently crept into a friend's backpack. I copied the number from the phone sex ad onto the Loebs' memo pad by their phone, ripped out the page, and took it home with me for later.

What followed after that night was a year of calls of my own into that phone-sex line, which I made from my bedroom when my parents weren't home. I spoke to at least a hundred different strangers from the Tri-State Area, describing myself, like Ronit did, as the girl I hoped I'd one day become. I made myself an art school student in her freshman year: sometimes I went to SVA and sometimes I went to NYU. I was wearing stockings. I was bare-legged. I had red hair with blond streaks in it and was "curvy, not chubby." I said I was nineteen or twenty-one, even though I was not yet old enough to get a learner's permit.

I spoke to all types—from the guy who said he looked like Kiefer Sutherland and lived on the Upper East Side, and that maybe we should get a coffee at Barney Greengrass, to the man with a snarly voice you'd think belonged behind bulletproof glass at an OTB, who told me about how much he'd like to rub my "clitty," which, to this day, remains the creepiest word I've ever heard in my life, ranking above strong contenders like "cunny," "diapey," and the term "pop-pop." I mastered the sequence of events that belie the exposition of any sex-themed conversation: outfit description and bullet points detailing one's physical appearance, command to one's phone partner to slide his/her underpants off and play with one's own genitals, and then, a detailed play-by-play of sex acts, starting at tit play and culminating in fuck-based ejaculation. I got good at it. And my formative phone sex experience is also responsible for the only orgasm I've ever faked in my life. I wanted to get off the phone in time for dinner (salmon croquettes!).

I'm good at keeping what I decide is a secret, so nobody ever found out. It was one of my suburban diversions—I wouldn't even tell Ronit. I kept it to myself. It was like Second Life, I guess, or whatever contemporary teenagers do on the Internet to pretend that they're not living through the most awkward years of their lives. I guess I didn't share the same sexual hang-ups as my peers, but whether that's chalk-uppable to being raised a healthy distance away from any sexual guilt or just being ravenous in general is anyone's guess. I just knew that masturbating along to a human voice describing the future was way more exciting than spreading my legs under a bath faucet and thinking about Dan Larroquette. And I got to meet people, sort of! It was almost like dating. All of a sudden, there were so many real men in my life in a fake way, and it didn't even occur to me that many of them were not who they said they were, just as I certainly wasn't who I said I was. I remember when one guy confided to me that he was married, and I was *shocked*. Wasn't phone sex cheating? I certainly wasn't eighteen with C-cups and a tiny ass, but at least I wasn't *attached*.

I learned a lot about men, and what sort of things they like to hear to get turned on. I figured out that the penetration and the violation of it all was the money shot—sex wasn't about food photography or college students on the beach. And just as some people will swear to you that a man's stomach is the best route to his heart, I was under the impression that the better I got at learning what titillated guys sexually, the closer I'd be to straddling my life goal of being in love with a guy who wanted a wife he wouldn't have to cheat on.

After a year or so, the novelty of calling into that number wore off. But at its best, my time on the phone allowed me to imagine a time in which I'd be sleeping with actual men who would gape at me the way they ogled *Penthouse* pets—or their actual sex partners—and do dirty things to me that we'd come up with together. It seemed like a far-off time from then, when I was beholden to Melissa and invisible to Yehuda, Josh, Ben, Eytan, and everybody else in my grade—even the kid who came dressed up as Spock every year for Purim. But hearing about sex, and talking about it, even to strangers, helped me practice for what I hoped would come soon, and be the real thing.

be your own gay best friend

"High School is fun," my mother lied to me in the kitchen one evening after dinner, rinsing plates. I was about to leave the Hebrew day school I'd attended from kindergarten through grade eight for the local public high school, and I had a sneaky feeling that the transition from small to big pond was going to be absolutely terrible. I didn't like change in general, and I worried that high school would be like the video for "Jeremy"—an overlit tableau of frozen pointers and laughers, with Eddie Vedder scatting over the whole affair.

There were things about high school I was looking forward to, but not many. I was eager to move on from the Jew womb (Joom?) I'd had my fill of. I was excited about no longer having a daily Hebrew language requirement or mandatory morning services, which I spent reading the parts of my prayer book that detailed concentration camp atrocities and fantasizing sexually about Steve Buscemi. Also, I figured, attending a new school with kids who never met me would give me a fresh start. Maybe I'd finally have an opportunity to promote myself from my current social rank of "sexually invisible." And at age fourteen, all I wanted to do was get laid. It was all I thought about, when I wasn't thinking about how cool it was to be agnostic, and how much I liked the Violent Femmes.

So, I trudged off to Scarsdale High School in my JCPenney jeans, penny loafers, and Eddie Bauer flannel shirt, unbuttoned over the Sub Pop Records T-shirt I'd bought in a men's Large from the back of Bleecker Bob's on a school field trip. I'd never even been French kissed, but now the backdrop was different. I was breaking ground on a new chapter of my life, and this one, I decided, would be sweet, effervescent, and a little dangerous— the Pop Rocks and Coca-Cola phase of my adolescence.

Well, it was all a big disaster. The opposite of fun. Sure, I got to first base my first year, with Jed, a redheaded junior so ugly I thought he was deformed at first. He did me the favor of sliding his fat, soft tongue into my mouth, while we, along with other drama club nerds, watched *Heathers*. The lights were down and I sat behind him, cross-legged, on the floor. He asked for a backrub, and I obliged, only to field a Linda Blair–style head turn from Jed, who made his move over his shoulder. He was gross, but there's something about open-mouth kissing, even with somebody who looks like the kid from *Mask*, that wires directly into your libido. Frenching is like the cross-shaped wood that connects with strings to the marionette that is your privates. I got immensely excited feeling Jed's mouth on and in mine, but declined when he asked if I wanted to go into the next room. Kissing this gargoyle in the dark, in a sea of other kids watching Winona Ryder and Shannen Doherty play croquet, made it easier for me to pretend it wasn't happening. If we went into the next room, I might have had to touch his penis, or see his face. But like so many hook-ups in the dark, the incident was never spoken of again.

The second time I made out with a boy was also the first time I gave a blowjob, and that was a far more magical, fantastical experience devoid of Christian Slater movies or a roomful of people who know all the words to *Miss Saigon*.

I was hanging out at the time with this girl Reneé, a Jersey goth chick who went to see *Rocky Horror* on Saturdays and listened to New Order. She and I made plans to go into the city together one night with her friend Nick, a kid she knew from *Rocky*. Nick was tall and thin and wore gray eyeliner, and I thought he was really sexy. He gave us a ride to the Knitting Factory on East Houston Street, where we drank vodka cranberries and watched musicians play free jazz while Nick and I groped each other's junk outside our respective pants. When we came back to Jersey, Reneé went into her house and Nick and I hopped into the backseat of his grandpa-style car—a Chevrolet or something. There was groping—I felt his finger dive past my tits and torso and sink into my vagina—and my mouth on his mouth, and then, my mouth on his dick. And here's the thing, reader. Here's where you have to cue the music that plays during the third act of *Full House*, when Danny Tanner sits DJ down and explains to her that who you are on the inside is what counts.

I remember thinking the moment I felt Nick's goth penis in my mouth that I. Was. *Home*. That this was what I was meant to do. It all felt so natural, so right. I imagine it was an experience that gay men relate to: the first time they suck a cock and cup a pair of balls, they hear bells. They just know exactly what to do. The guy is so happy. You're so happy. My own thumb, which I'd sucked until the embarrassingly late age of twelve, had finally found its glorious replacement. *Hallelujah!* I thought. *This is who I am!*

After Nick, every time I got the opportunity to make out in high school, I felt like guys were doing *me* a favor letting me suck them off; like I was the one who deserved high fives afterward, because I enjoyed it. Ben Spiegel took me upstairs to his parents' guest room during a Friday night kegger and took out his angry, purple cock from the fortress of his 501s, and I acted like I'd been elected student-body president. "You like me! You really like me!" But after sloppy third, I rarely spoke to any of those guys. It wasn't because I didn't like them anymore; it was because once it was over, they weren't seeking anything more. It was a pattern I got used to, even though I always wanted to hook up again. Just as my favorite style of dress is "new," my favorite kind of sexual activity, at least at the time, was "more."

AFTER THAT peen parade had marched through my mouth and the street workers had swept up the copious ticker tape in its wake, my sex life in high school shriveled up and killed itself. The blowjob party of ninth grade was pretty much the majority of the action I got in high school, and I blame the A-School for that. I transferred to the Scarsdale Alternative School, or "The A-School," after my freshman year. SAS is a subset of the high school not for the behaviorally challenged, but instead for the progressive-emotionally-minded. And that decision begat an unequivocal disaster—a real didgeri-*don't*. I blame hippies for everything, but most of all for preventing me from getting laid until college.

The A-School was cozy and hands-on, with its fuzzy learning techniques and nosy, socialist-minded procedures seemingly designed for the sole purpose of making me angry all the time. We sat on the floor and called our math teacher "Cheryl." We held community meetings every Wednesday and confronted one another for smoking pot before Spanish. Classes were small and teachers doubled as advisors. If you seemed like you were in a bad mood, they'd confront you about it, or ask you rhetorically how you thought your actions were affecting the community. It was like est, but they let you pee. A lot of people wore Patagonias and hiking boots, and everybody seemed to have a Phish sticker on his SUV.

This environment is precisely where I lost my mind. It seemed like some kind of sick experiment, finding myself in the company of self-designated flower children of the upper middle class while I grappled with hormones that made me at once angrier and hornier than I'd ever been in my life. I hated everybody around me so much, and at the same time, wanted to have sex with them.

Alas, I was not sporting the most approachable, sensual look at the time. I shopped the more esoteric sections of the Salvation Army for postal-service uniforms I'd pair with T-shirts that commemorated christenings of babies I did not know. I circled the "A" when signing my last name so it made an anarchy symbol. I wore a chain wallet. I tenaciously sought out all things "counterculture," including small-press publishing, true-crime literature, home recording, "outsider" art created by the mentally ill, and at least three other areas of interest strategically designed to alienate myself from other A-Schoolers. Nobody in their right mind would have tried to fuck my mouth; they'd be too scared of getting their dicks bitten off.

There were a couple of fluke hook-ups beyond the Ginger-headed Frencher, Purple Dick, and the Rocky Horror Picture Blow. They were hippies, mostly. A bong-hitter with a frizzy ponytail who used to bring his wah-wah pedal to jam sessions at the A-School Fair took me to a construction site off Heathcote Road one night, then came on my leg in the back of his Saab. He dumped me later that week after giving me a ride to school in icy silence, the humiliation of which hurt only until I saw him shotgun a cheerleader at a party after she took a hit from a skull bong.

There was Eddie Ashe, one of those drama-club guys who wears fedoras and trenchcoats, whom I met at Tower Video. Eddie had complicated, feathered hair, and I thought he was really cool until he suffered a panic attack after ejaculating in his chinos while we made out to *Glengarry Glenn Ross*. Another tip-off that Eddie may not have been cool was his incessant talking about how much he *loved* the sweet, funky sounds of the bass guitar. He forced me to give Les Claypool "props," and listen to that band Fishbone before suffering one final flip-out in front of me, after the Glengarry Cum Pants incident, during which he wondered if he was "maybe not scared of rejection as much as scared of, you know, acceptance?"

There was a boy from New Rochelle who felt my boobs in the vestibule of a diner, near the chalky dinner mints and the lotto-scratch-ticket machines. He smelled like tuna fish and had a mushroom haircut, but I convinced myself I was in love with him as I watched him skateboard away, unaware it was the last time I'd ever see him.

Taking these guys' tongues in my mouth, even moments before being sloppily jilted, was sweet, distilled ecstasy. Making out brought me into another state of consciousness, even though I was just getting Grade-D play from sixteen-year-old wankers with dancing bears stickered to their rear windows. But when it didn't work out because of myriad *duh*-fueled reasons, I was devastated. Furious. How dare he?! I hate myself! All-or-nothing stuff, with too much rage and too little perspective. You're familiar: you were an adolescent too.

When I think today about what it was like to be a teenager, I want to go back in time just to put a warm washcloth on my fifteen-year-old forehead and hold my own hand. I have a weak spot for any movie that shows a character's adult self going back to reassure herself as a child, including but not limited to *Drop Dead Fred*. Seriously: I will cry like a *baby* when I see old Phoebe Cates reassuring young Phoebe Cates that everything will be all right. I think it's because I really do want to go back and tell myself that the good things about me will stay the same, and the bad things will change.

Of all the things that have changed, the biggest difference between me now and me then is that, when I was a teenager, I didn't seem to have a sense of humor. Even in my silly thrift-shop clothes, obsessively taping episodes of *SCTV* and *Saturday Night Live*, nothing was funny about my own life to me—which is what it *really* means to have a sense of humor, comedy nerds.

And do you know why it is I didn't have a sense of humor? It's something I've figured out only recently. I was such a miserable sack of humorless gristle because I was, at the time, without a Single. Gay. Friend.

I AM always suspicious of women who aren't friends with at least a few gay men; it doesn't speak well to their wit, glamour, cultural tastes, or whether it's fun to be around them at all. It's imperative that women keep the company of at least one gay man, not only because they make the best friends you'll ever keep, but because the alternatives have built-in leaks. Straight male friends are mostly guys you want to sleep with or want something from professionally, and straight female friendships are incapable of *not* being wrought with jealousy and drama. Show me a woman who doesn't have at least two former best girlfriends she now hates, and I will introduce you to a convincing tranny.

Gay men appreciate what is feminine about women, and what is funny about being feminine, which is why they appreciate funny women, and bring out the sense of humor in girls more than anybody else on earth. It is extremely important to be friends with at least one gay man, and even more so when you are in high school. If yours is the sad fate of growing up in a part of the country in which the word "fag" is used by popular kids as liberally as freshly ground pepper is by bistro waiters—or, even worse, if you are too dull to retain the interest of the smartly dressed boy in your AP history class who calls Margaret Thatcher "fierce"—then you need to learn to be your *own* gay best friend. It is the only thing that will keep you from going insane, or possibly cutting yourself, which is a cowardly plea for attention and unsightly at the beach.

Looking back, I should have been more diligent in finding a homosexual companion. I should have been Chasing Gary that whole time, instead of throwing myself at Wah-Wah Pedal and Riff Raff. My Hypothetical Gay Best Friend would have changed my outlook on my whole situation. Sure, high school was horrible and gross, and the people I went to school with, for the most part, were fugly and retarded. But what if, instead of saying to yourself over and over: "That Amy Shelov is such a dipshit—she's never heard of the *Galapagos Islands*? What a dumb slut. I hope she gets hit by a bus," you had the singsong sarcasm of a wry male voice cracking wise: "Wow. Amy Shelov seems really cool. You should be more like her."

I'm not big on regret—until time travel actually exists, it seems like a waste of making yourself feel bad—but I do wish I'd played hag to my own invisible wise, gay, companion in high school; my Jiminy Faggot. I'd have kept him on my shoulder during homeroom, shushing him merrily as he complimented the teacher for wearing the same reindeer sweater two days in a row. I'd have been able to listen to his droll sniping instead of my righteous vitriol every time some Deadhead said something asinine.

And I would have had somebody around to remind me, when I was sobbing into a tuna sub while parked behind the Borders Books in the Westchester Pavilion, that things were going to one day get better. Nobody knows about the promise of a new day better than gay people and Paula Abdul. It's what gets closeted, picked-on queer kids through junior high—the hope that around the bend, you'll be living in a major city, pulling in disposable income from your media job, fucking a gorgeous guy who loves you, and hanging out with people who went through the same thing you did and lived to tell about it. That there's a time that exists when you can be who you are, and who you are is fabulous. I really needed to know that, then.

I HAD to wait until college to meet my best friend; the homosexual who would complete me. Nate came along my junior year, not a moment too soon, and taught me it's more satisfying to laugh at idiots than to spend hours plotting their doom. Like me, he came from similarly embarrassing stock: Nate had long hair in high school, went vegan, chained himself to trees, and dressed up like Evil Ronald McDonald for a Greenpeace protest. He understood that only those who've been balls-deep in super-earnest ideology are really able to laugh heartily in the faces of its most orthodox devotees. It's just a question of growing out of being sad all the time. And Nate and I had some satisfying belly laughs at the expense of the raw-foodists, transgender feminists, anticonsumerist performance artists, and assorted other East Village clucks we lived among once we'd finally found each other at NYU, in the belly of the beast. It felt so good to make fun of people for once, instead of silently hating them.

I told Nate about this time in September, after the summer between my sophomore and junior years, when I decided I was going to dress like a beatnik from then on, and showed up to high school in a black beret, clutching a copy of *Howl* like a purse. Talking to him made it all suddenly seem really funny, and not like I was airing out a sanctimonious confession of how miserable I used to be. It was such a relief. I wish Nate had been with me the whole time when I was hurting and sweating every last piece of flotsam and jetsam that sideswiped me in high school. It would have been a blessing to be reminded, in the trenches of tenth grade, that I was Kate Pierson, not Aileen Wuornos.

Nate and I made up for all the time I lost when I was in high school hanging out with nobody, and dum-dums. We'd commiserate with each other when stupid boys would disappear after making us fall for them. Girlfriends will give you a hug and a pep talk when that happens—gay friends will merrily and artfully tear the guy to pieces, pointing out his awful haircut, his terrible clothes, and the love handles you didn't notice when you still had a crush on him. It's very comforting to have a boy be that mean to another boy when your heart is broken, and Nate and I made merciless fun of all the people we dated who didn't work out.

I'D KEEP detailing the various ways in which Nate and I have made each other laugh and generally enjoyed each other's company over the years, but I'm afraid you, as I, would want to heap generous loads of hot barf on your own lap. There's something essentially revolting about stories about fun that was had or "you had to be there" accounts of the hilarious thing that guy did that time that end with, "We were laughing so hard, we couldn't breathe." They're like the "Wow, that party last night was so fun!" kind of anecdotes. So, I'll stop.

But Nate was the kind of present you get from someplace good, like *Tiffany & Co.* or the *SkyMall* catalog, and I felt like I could finally relax once he came along; like he was a harbinger of all good things, coming soon. I wish I could go back, *Drop Dead Fred* style, and tell Ol' Teenage Beatnik Me that soon enough she'd burst from her emo chrysalis to attract wonderful gay guys from all walks of life. I'd introduce her to Nate and his boyfriend, and tell her that I'd one day be in the company of the most intelligent, funny, and culturally well-versed people in the world, who totally got me and loved me unconditionally. That I'd have friends like him who were actually rooting for me to find love and success and weren't looking to undermine my efforts with their own intentions, like girlfriends can do. And if the crabby teenager version of me still wouldn't stop pouting, I'd defer to Nate, who would tell her that at least I stopped sucking hippie cock before my twenties started. That ought to shut her up.

twin cities

W hen I was fifteen years old, I began exchanging letters and phone calls with a seventeen-year-old boy named Tom, who lived in Eden Prairie, Minnesota. Tom was funny and charming in a way I wasn't familiar with, and he gave me a glimpse into that distinctly Midwestern kind of polite awkwardness. Friendly with a twist of something missing; warm with a gust of cold. Tom and I connected nerdily on the Internet when it was still budding and dewy, like peach fuzz on a newborn's hiney, during one of the loneliest times I remember being alive.

I WAS new to high school and desperate to make friends at the time, so I joined the Women's Issues Club, whose after-school meetings offered various activities fueled by feminist intention. For example, one afternoon we would look for sexist ads in fashion magazines and write letters in ballpoint pen on note-book paper to the calculating Neanderthals behind the offensive Love's Baby Soft "beautiful girls wear our perfume" campaign. And other times, we would just eat chips and complain.

One girl from the club, Reem, walked with a cane and had coarse, woolly hair she wore in a ponytail that lay slack atop the enormous backpack she strapped to both shoulders. She was Lebanese and misanthropic and she liked industrial music and puns. Reem was also one of the first people I met who was interested in the Web in its early stages. She was vir-tuosic with Prodigy e-mail, Netscape browsers, and Usenet, a message board with newsgroups for people around the world who shared common interests, like sci-fi and avoiding parties.

Reem had met her long-distance boyfriend, Duncan, from a newsgroup devoted to the band Throbbing Gristle. Duncan, a thin, Tim Burton stop-motion puppet of a boy, was moving to New York from Michigan to attend SVA after meeting Reem IRL (in real life) and falling hard. I was intrigued by the idea of the Internet as a shopping destination for a long-distance-turned-real-life boyfriend, and, as I mentioned, desperate to make friends, because fifteen is the worst age for everybody in the world to be, unless you are Miley Cyrus.

Reem invited me to her house one day after school, and together we dicked around with her computer. She showed me postings from the Usenet groups she subscribed to, and I asked her whether there was a newsgroup for They Might Be Giants, my favorite band at the time. Nerd alert? Oh, *you bet*. In retro-spect, asking whether They Might Be Giants had an early Web presence is like asking Tom Sizemore if he could introduce you to a prostitute.

Reem pulled up a screen, then scooted aside as I hungrily perused the musings of similarly affectioned geeks across the nation. Before the Internet, I was hitting the microfiche to get my geek fix, printing out obsession-relevant articles in blue-gray ink from the archives of the Public Library. But now I was being exposed to an online community that offered instant access to both information and *similarly minded fans!* Quarts of dopamine flooded the tissues of my lizard brain.

I begged Reem to print out posts from three threads of my choosing on her old-fashioned printer paper with the holes on both sides so I could take the Internet home with me and read it in bed. Kind, Lebanese, awkward, acne-plagued, Duncan-beloved Reem did just that. And at home, I pored over those posts like I was looking for a job.

I found something better. One of the guys from the news-group, this fellow Tom from Minnesota, had weighed in on a thread and closed his communication with a quote from a *Kids in the Hall* sketch. I got his reference all the way from Scarsdale and nearly fell out of my bed in paroxysms of camaraderie.

The notion of finding another human being who liked not just one, but both of the two demographically similar institutions that I was dorkily obsessed with at the time was an epiphany. What were the odds of these two perfect human qualities converging in a Venn Diagram of romantic compatibility?! Wait a minute—he's black, *and* he can dance?

Tom was the invisible boyfriend I wanted in high school. Even though I'd hook up from time to time, and I thought I wanted to be in a relationship more than anything, I don't think I was ready for a real person to sop up my time. There were too many laps for me to drive around Central Avenue and tag sales for me to troll for vintage cookbooks that I could cut up for collages; all solo activities. Tom was perfect because he was a fantasy at half a country's distance. I was beginning to learn that long-distance relationships are an exciting, fun way for your brain to masturbate.

During the school day, I'd jot down things to chat about with Tom on the phone later that evening. I went into our conversations with bullet points, knowing our time was metered; this was during the pre-Skype, Candace Bergen-for-Sprint's dime-a-minute calling plan days. So, my dad would bug me about the phone bill and Tom and I would keep it brief. And after hanging up, I'd take to my pad, my pen, and the post office, and the two of us forged a lovely bit of old-timey correspondence back and forth, like Emily Dickinson and Thomas Wentworth Higginson, but if the two of them mainly talked about *Mystery Science Theater 3000.*

Tom was dry; friendly but reserved, and rather affectless. He wasn't in the business of lavishing attention on a tall poppy; his was the character of the gardener hired to prune it, out of courtesy to the rest of the flowers. I've since met other Midwesterners, and I know the drill: They can be witty, bright, and kind, but they're not self-centered, grandiose, or emotional. They are even-tempered, even during shitstorms of winter weather that render their climate unfit for life. They use relative negatives when they're asked how they're doing, and say they "could be worse." They're polite enough to keep their feelings from bleeding over into messy ethnic territories. They hate margarine.

Most of what I knew about Minnesotans was gleaned from the movie *Fargo*, which came out after Tom and I forged our long-distance friendship. There's a scene in that film in which

Frances McDormand's character, Marge Gunderson, is reunited with an Asian guy named Mike Yanagita she used to go to high school with. Mike saw Marge "on the tee vee," and wanted to meet at the Radisson Hotel in Minneapolis to have lunch, while Marge was in town on business. After forced small talk, Mike oversteps his boundaries and comes around to sit next to Marge on her side of the table. Marge, unsure if Mike is hitting on her, politely asks him to go back to his own booth, and that's when he breaks down. Mike sobs to Marge that he lost his wife to cancer but how he always thought Marge was such a "super lady." They decide to meet "maybe another time, then," and Marge determinedly sips Diet Coke through her mixer straw as a defense to the crippling awkwardness of inappropriate be-havior from a lovesick stranger.

After months of chatting in high school, I was smitten with what I knew and didn't know about Tom. I loved his wry sense of humor, his bordering-on-Canadian accent, his coy withholding of any indicative affection toward me beyond our phone conversations about TV shows and music we did or didn't like. It was a perfect fifteen-year-old not-romance. Until he ended it one day, after I told him I loved him. He was Marge, I was Mike Yanagita.

"Er . . . well, I suppose I'm sorry, but I don't feel the same way about you," said a neutral voice from a sturdy teenager of Nordic descent, coming from the earpiece of my bedroom phone.

I was devastated. And of course, asshandedly back-headed to use the L-word in the first place. And not the L-word that references that show about ladies who love pomade. I used the one that describes what *everybody* wants.

So Tom dissolved, and that was that for a while. I

meandered toward other imaginary boyfriends I could pro-
fess my love to, but they were mostly photos in magazines of
Michael Keaton in *Batman Returns* and white-turtleneck-and-
aviator glasses-clad-early-70s-era Mike Nesmith. It wasn't until
fifteen years later, a full twice my time on the planet since I'd
first stumbled upon Tom's Usenet ID, that I decided to look
him up. This was last summer.

SINCE TOM was an Internet early adopter, he was easily Google-
able. I found his blog, which, like our phone conversations at
the time, mostly documented music he liked and the shows
he watched. But I also gawked at the photos he posted of his
family, because it turned out, he had one. Tom was married and
had two little girls. Everybody looked robust and happy, and
his kids had his eyes. He wrote about his and his wife's efforts
to lose weight, commemorated his girls' birthdays, and posted
wedding photos. I felt like a creepy tourist sifting through his
personal information, however public he made it by putting
it up on his blog. My blog mostly has plugs for my shows and
sometimes I'll post a YouTube video I find of a cat answering
an office phone (julieklausner.com!).

I lapsed into callous New Yorker mode looking at Tom's
photos and summoned my sneering superiority, which is
a reflex. In some respects, even though it had been forever
since he and I had last spoken, I was still basking in that catty
schadenfreude you get when you see somebody who once rejected you, looking less than Daniel Craig–like in the physical-
attractiveness department. But a blog post Tom wrote on his
wedding anniversary cut my smirking short. Its title was "8th
Anniversary," and its text read, simply: "If you get a chance,
marry your best friend. Totally worth it."

I cried actual tears when I read that. Not because some-body else had nabbed the one who got away—the one who was never mine nor here—but because this guy was in love and I was *not*! Jealousy always trumps schadenfreude! It's a rule from the heartbreak version of "rock, paper, scissors."

So, for my thirtieth birthday last year, I decided to fly to Minneapolis. I wanted to meet Tom. Fine, I also wanted to go to the Mall of America. But mostly, I wanted to meet this stranger with a family; the one I spoke to all the time in my bedroom grotto half my life ago. I decided we should meet for drinks in the bar at the Radisson Hotel, like Mike and Marge.

"It seems to be the place for awkward reunions," Tom agreed in an e-mail.

Nate, who agreed to accompany me on the trip after I promised him we'd get our old-timey photos taken at the Mall, watched TV in our hotel room while I made my way down to the Radisson bar, wearing a nipple-concealing scarf over a tight white tank top and a fetching pencil skirt with a peacock print. I was certain I looked brake-screechingly cosmopolitan. I expected Tom's brain to crumble like an Entenmann's treat in the wake of my fashion forwardness.

He didn't care. Soon after I arrived at the bar, I got a hand-shake and a hug from a tall, wide, living, breathing version of the photo of a young man with a Dwight Eisenhower haircut I'd been mailed years ago.

"It's nice to meet you," Tom said.

He was curt and rehearsed and clearly weirded-out. I was too, but I'd fueled my anxiety into hyper-friendliness, if only as an exercise in contrast. I'd say Tom was slow to warm, but I'm not sure he ever did. At least he made eye contact with me after finishing his second beer, curbing my "Wow, so there's the

Mary Tyler Moore statue" pleasantries with a blunt "Let's start from the beginning." He told me where he went to college, and how he met his wife his second day at school, married her, and then had kids. He told me about his tech job, about his in-laws, and that he doesn't get to go see live bands as much as he used to, now that he's a dad. So far, I could have been anybody. This was just his bio. I was aching for the kind of self-referential conversation that fuels any one-on-one exchange I'd ever been half of, whether it was on a date or at a job interview. This is what I'm about; how about you? But Tom didn't ask me any questions, so I just decided to start talking about myself. My angle was: "I'm awesome!"

I gave him an overview of my career, and filled him in on my life in New York; my friends, my accomplishments. I asked if he'd seen any of my work online. He hadn't. As guilty as I felt spying on his blog, I was sort of surprised—even insulted—that he didn't have the reciprocal curiosity to cyber-stalk me (julie klausner.com!). But I plowed forward, looking not so much for approval, but for some semblance of common ground. I asked him if he'd ever been to New York, and he hadn't. He said he went to Vegas one time when he was getting good at online poker, and mentioned something about a strip club in passing, which made me feel gross. All of a sudden, Tom felt like a long-lost brother to me, and nobody wants to think of their brother with a stripper's tits in his face.

I made a point of outlining the difference between our relationship situations. I told Tom in a matter-of-fact way, that people my age in Manhattan don't tend to get married in our early twenties. That we get our careers figured out first and shop around for the right person. I was telling that to myself as much as him. He seemed perplexed.

"But what if you meet the right person at a young age?" he asked. It was like fielding questions from a caveman about outer space.

Then he asked what music I'd been listening to lately. I had to break the news to Tom that I didn't follow new music as voraciously as I did when he knew me. That I sort of stopped caring about new bands shortly after alternative music became indie rock and an internship I did at Matador Records made me realize that I didn't want to spend any more of my time hanging out with the kind of people who seem to love those records than I absolutely had to. And then, soon after that, how a band called The Sea and Cake came around, and how the tweeness of that indie-jazz fuckery indelibly alienated me from anything I ever wanted to do with new music again. How what was once crunchy and weird and fun to discover with partners in crime had become alienating and pretentious and competitive and exclusionary. And that around that time, I started getting bored of going to rock shows and found more pleasure listening to the cast recording of *Jesus Christ Superstar* in my apartment than standing around at a club holding my winter coat and a beer in a plastic cup. By the time I met Tom in person, I was no longer the teenage girl who pored through the pages of the new *Magnet* or *Paste* magazine, starving for a fix from the new verse-chorus-verse ensemble. I was over it, and I had new things on my plate I wanted to talk about.

My answer made Tom's face fall.

"That makes me sad," he said. "You really introduced me to some of my favorite music that I still listen to today."

I didn't take this the way Tom intended it. All I heard him say was, "You've changed. You used to be cool." And that really pissed me off. This guy never knew me; he was just connecting, as men tend to do, with the emotional veracity of the songs he learned to associate with me at the time.

I wonder if music is more important to guys, or if they just process it differently. Why they have an impulse to catalog it and chart their tastes; to talk bands the way little boys trade baseball cards. I look back at my hunger for that kind of talk as a teenager, and I wonder if it echoed my hopes of getting inside the male mind, the way I ate up those porno magazines. I love music, but I don't get a singular thrill hearing a needle graze vinyl, and I hate more than anything conversation about bands people go to see, and how hard they rocked.

So when Tom said that, I tried not to seem insulted and quickly returned to my talking points. "I'm so happy about my career. I perform a lot. I write for TV sometimes!" But when you talk to a person with a family about how great your professional life is, all you're doing is accenting the divide. You're not making them even a tiny bit jealous about what they're missing at home in the arms of their spouse, surrounded by their progeny. You're just driving it home: "You and I have major differences that will become insurmountable upon repetition." Tom didn't care about my career any more than I cared about what songs he had on his iPod, and dropping names to him of celebrities I'd worked with was like telling a dog that you lost five pounds. The dog doesn't care. He's listening for the word "walk" and waiting for you to make your way over to the food bowl. The rest is white noise.

Tom and I drank and caught up for two hours, at which point he volunteered to drive me around for a tour of the Twin Cities. I told him I had to meet Nate for dinner, which was true. But I also backed out because my street smarts kicked in. I was reluctant to get into a car alone with a person I didn't know. And that's when I really saw Tom for who he was: a stranger. A friendly stranger with whom I shared at least one experience IRL, and one who was probably unlikely to abduct and torture me with duct tape and electrical wire—but also, in distilled truth, a man I didn't know, who lives in a strange place.

So, I politely declined Tom's offer and we said our goodbyes. I told him to let me know if he ever made his way to New York, and he said he'd keep in touch this time.

I WENT upstairs, and Nate asked me how it went; who he was and if we'd hit it off. I told him I wasn't sure; that I didn't know whether I liked Tom or not. It's like how you don't even think about whether or not you like the guy who works a floor below you. Still, I wonder what he thought of me. I'm obsessed with being liked, even by children and people I don't know: sadly, it's one of the symptomatic motivations of anyone in a creative profession. And I didn't get any signs from Tom one way or the other until, I got back to New York.

A few days after our Radisson rendezvous, Tom sent me an e-mail that said "Thanks" in the subject header. I read his note and remembered how charming he could be in his written correspondences. He thanked me for "being bold" and getting together, and told me how glad he was to reconnect. Then he launched into a laundry list of Netflix movies he'd just seen and TV shows he'd caught up on since I gave him recommendations over drinks. He told me about some podcasts he thought I should check out and gave me a list of movies his kids liked. And then he sent me a link to an online compilation of songs he'd put together for my benefit, to catch me up on what he'd been listening to in the last few years. It was an overdue mix tape, and I liked almost all the songs he chose. It meant a lot that he'd selected that music with me in mind, and it gave me a belated relief knowing how it felt, at least for him, to finally meet me.

He even gave my playlist a title: "Super Lady."

SECTION TWO

missing knuckles, snowballing vegans, self-help books, and other atrocities

"Doing what you want to do is not always in your best interest."

—*The Rules*

"Nobody invites a bad-looking idiot up to their bedroom."

—*Broadcast News*

the rules

Hey! Remember the '90s?

The Clintons were in office, everybody was using AOL, Will Ferrell and Cheri Oteri did "The Cheerleaders" on *SNL*, and everybody thought Oasis was fantastic.

In hindsight, we were all a bunch of potato-salad-eating jackasses. Sure, it was before 9/11, and optimism always looks like corn-shucking yokelry before planes hit buildings, but we were also marinating in the guava juices of our own naïveté, having collectively just hit our national stride of financial prosperity. And nothing lends itself more to navel-gazing than having a surplus of money and time on one's hands. Appropriately enough, it was in the mid-90s when I began my liberal arts college education.

I went to NYU's Gallatin School of Individualized Study, a school I'd chosen because of my crippling fear of places that are not New York City and Gallatin's decidedly laissez-faire policy about what you actually had to learn. My self-designed concentration was in "Cultural Criticism," which afforded me the freedom to take classes in filmmaking, postmodern literature, abnormal sexual behavior, social psychology, dramatic writing, performance studies, and arts journalism. Gallatin called itself "The School Without Walls," and you know what it *also* didn't really have? A lot of practical requirements for graduation. You had to take one math *or* science credit, and social science counted as a science. It was sort of like the A-School: Part Two, only at Gallatin, nobody cared about you. I spent three evenings and two afternoons a week in three-hour classes, discussing whether gender was a construct, and I had the rest of my week to spend browsing Wet Seal and looking for guys to fall in love with.

The other defining memory I have of the mid-1990s was that everybody seemed to be talking about dating all the goddamn time.

The Rules, that shrill creed designed to make women feel bad about their own desires, was published in 1995. *The First Wives Club* came out the year after. Then, in 1998, the Monica Lewinsky scandal broke, and *Sex and the City* debuted. I think 1997 is the only respite of the zeitgeist chatter concerning the ins and outs of romance, and I blame that on Princess Diana's death. Clearly, a nation's vaginas were sitting shiva on the behalf of the People's Princess.

At this time, I, too, was eager, to paraphrase Morgan Freeman in *The Shawshank Redemption,* playing (for a change) a wise old black man, to "get busy datin' or get busy dyin'." I bought into the Clintonian promise of a mouth for every dick, and I wanted in on the deal. The rest of the world seemed to buzz on the same frequency, and women everywhere in New York City seemed to crawl with dating desperation. Terminology that previously only lived between the covers of *Cosmo* now seemed to be inescapable: Get and keep a man! Commitment time! Pleasure zones! On the prowl!

I dressed the part, in animal prints and red lipstick. But I wasn't going for "cougar"—I wanted to do the B-movie, cat-eye-glasses, Bettie Page, fishnets, and Russ Meyer thing. You know, the look that people in the Pacific Northwest still think is really cutting-edge? But it didn't look cute on me. Instead, I looked like a woman with designs on men, and more Delta Burke than Annie Potts.

Predictably, my efforts were tempered by the fact that real life, thank God, is nothing like *Cosmo* magazine. Which is why nobody should wear makeup to the gym to meet men or learn how to perfect one's "Faux-O." I was like Carrie Bradshaw only in that I hung out downtown and wanted a boyfriend. My shoes were limited to a couple of comfortable options, I didn't drink, and you couldn't see my collarbone without an MRI. Also, the people I hung out with around that time were pretty un-fabulous.

There was Jodi, my roommate from New Jersey who was missing a set of knuckles, so her fingers could only go perpendicular. Candace, the only person I ever met to have actually grown up in the Orchard Beach section of the Bronx, who used to strip to Motley Crüe in Yonkers and blamed her small breasts on an eating disorder she developed during puberty. And Eve, a dumpster-diving punk-rocker wannabe whose identification of water as "wudder" screamed "Pennsylvania Mainline," but who wanted more than anything to live in a squat somewhere in 1982. Eve's whole life was scored by *URGH! A Music War*, but her bank account was padded with the wages of comfortable suburban parents. I was also friendly with a lot of gay girls who would never get sick of telling me how great Judith Butler's books are, and why it was important to see *Boys Don't Cry* more than once, "to catch the subtleties."

"I don't get it," said Lauryn, one of the aforementioned lesbians, after I made the mistake of asking her for advice about my sorry dating life. "How many times are you going to get screwed over by all those shitty guys before you move on?"

I just giggled in response, like she was flirting with me—all gay people who share your gender want to have sex with you, you know—and thought, "Lauryn's so funny!" I knew sex with a girl was like the Master Cleanse: Maybe it changed other people's lives for the better, but it wasn't for me, and it sort of made my stomach hurt a little to think about diving into that particular collegiate cliché.

But Lauryn was right about the shitty guys. I dated them in college like it was my major.

I MET all grades of awful men getting picked up in bars I got into with a fake Georgia driver's license. Under the guise of hailing from Savannah, I got to meet winners like Reginald Blankenship, a carrot-topped lanky Kentuckian who met me at Max Fish two hours before requesting oral sex with a mint-flavored condom, which is sort of like ordering a cheeseburger and drinking it through a straw. Reginald taught me two things: that I can't be intimate with a man with the same skin and hair coloring as me, because the minute a redheaded man lowers his drawers, I feel like I'm looking at myself with male genitalia;

and also, that when you try to suck a guy off with a mint bal-
loon on his penis, he will ask you to stop, and then he will tell
you that he wants to take a bath.

I met a guy old enough to have known better than to
dabble with a college freshman at the now-defunct Coney Is-
land High on St. Mark's Place. We kissed until my hair caught
fire from the candle on the bar, igniting instantly the helmet of
White Rain hair spray I used to encase my ginger dome before
a night on the town. After the bartender did me the favor of
throwing a lager on my head, the dabbler and I had boring,
missionary sex. I remember his apartment was on Park Avenue
in the high 20s, and that he had photos of African children
on his wall. I wore a garter belt and stockings under what I
thought was a classy zebra-print skirt and V-neck top from
Express, and I moaned appreciatively as he gently plowed my
soft, eighteen-year-old body.

There was a boy at a hotel in Italy—a fellow American
traveler—whom I met over breakfast during a summer abroad.
I marveled at his chin-length Shirley Temple ringlets and tiny,
round balls for the time it took for him to finish in one of
Tuscany's finest lambskin condoms, only to run into him the
next day on the steps of some beautiful ruin in Rome, where
he told me he shouldn't meet up with me again, because he
was in a relationship back at home. "Me too," I lied back, feeling so stupid about being dumped abroad that I forgot *he* was
the one who transgressed. My wanting another night of what I
thought was good sex with a cute guy who happened to have
Bette Davis's hair from *Whatever Happened to Baby Jane* was still
less embarrassing than a guy thinking that just once, on vacation, wasn't cheating.

I didn't even like any of these guys, but I wanted so badly

for them to want me. When nobody called, I turned to the annals of self-help and dating books, ubiquitous as they were at the time. But I read them with an ingenious filter: I wouldn't listen to *anybody*.

"DON'T CALL Him and Rarely Return His Calls," advised Ellen Fein and Sherrie Schneider in Rule Number 5 of their dating book about not pursuing men in order to trick them into marrying you. I think the only book that made me as mad as *The Rules* was *The Atkins Bible*. I lasted on a low-carb diet for thirty seconds before losing my mind, and I didn't even try to follow any of "The Rules," even the ones that made sense, like "Don't Try to Change Him." Not going after what I wanted more than anything seemed counterintuitive to everything else I knew about the way things worked. If I wanted an internship, I'd pester higher and lower-ups at the office until I got it. If I wanted to get into a class, I'd show up at the Registrar at seven a.m., bounding through pedestrian traffic to calls of "Run, Forrest, Run!" from passersby in order to make it to the top of the queue on time. And when I had a crush on a boy, I would raze fields of wheat with a torch if I had to, in hopes of getting touch. I would call frequently and obsessively return his calls. I would ask him out. I would bring him gifts. Pay for meals. I would never end a date first, or without some sort of action. And as for Rule Number 3, "Don't Stare at Men or Talk Too Much"? Well, I was a gaping, chatting, rushing-into-sex monster, and the idea of seeming unavailable, when in fact I was desperate and ripe, ran counter to every instinct I ever had: that doing something, not nothing, was the way to get what you wanted from the world.

Predictably, the men I met who liked being chased were

will-o'-the-wisps and androgynous paupers. Boys who worked at bookstores, with no body hair or love handles; virgins and vegetarians, steampunk DIY'ers who peddled vintage and did Bikram Yoga. None of them could compete; none were formidable or compatible. Sex with that lot was lousy and awkward or never came to pass, and nobody was calling me, or calling me back.

Merrily I devoured fuel for my one-woman war against mating protocol, reading book after book featuring variations on the economic principle of supply and demand. And then came *He's Just Not That Into You*, which provided women the tremendous relief of knowing that they were simply not terribly *liked* by the objects of their affections.

I took umbrage with the idea that if he didn't call, he wasn't "into you"—that any guy who was in his right mind would know, if he liked a girl, how to chase her down until she was his. But what about the guys who *weren't* in their right minds? The ones who were a little off or lost, or damaged from past experiences, or had no clue that they were supposed to chase a girl down like a hound on a scent? That book made the assumption that if a guy didn't do what he should, even if he liked you just fine, then you didn't want him anyway.

But what if there turns out to be a *lot* of guys who don't know what to do? And what if you meet one and you know he's screwed up—like he'd been messed up to the point where he seems like an abused stray, whether it's the kind that snaps at you or cowers—but you like him enough to take him home with you anyway? What if you thought you could change him or teach him how to treat you, or you just wanted to enjoy the good parts of him and ignore the bad ones until someone better came along?

THAT WAS where I was, making the best of the turkeys in my path. And never did hearing that the guys I dated didn't actually like me ever provide comfort. That book was a sneaky way of reminding women that they don't like the way they're treated by guys who may in fact be perfectly "into them," but are otherwise dysfunctional. Because if a guy who knows what to do isn't *into you*, you don't need a book to tell you that. You get dumped or blown off after he pursues you like a contender, and then it hurts like crazy, because you know you lost out on someone who knew what to do.

But when you're young, and you're habitually dating the damaged, and they don't come through, you have to make the conscious choice to separate the columns in your head that say "This is who I am" and "This is how I am being treated." And then you have to figure out how to let go of somebody who's gone, not because you're pacified in the realization that you're not liked, but because you figure out that maybe you're the one who doesn't like *him*. Not just how he acts, but who he is. And then you have to decide if you want to keep going out with guys you *don't* think are great, or if you like yourself enough to hang out for a while on your own.

In no way was I in that place yet. I didn't like myself that much, and I certainly didn't want to be alone. I needed to make my own mistakes to learn from, and I wanted to see more of what was out there—even if it was ugly.

power of three

There was something a little off about Ryan. He didn't seem Nike Cult/BTK Killer/Octomom–crazy, but something about him was not quite right. Maybe it was that he slept under his friend's foosball table every night. Maybe it was his assortment of nervous tics, his clipped speech, his random laughter. Maybe it was his occasional, instance-inappropriate intensity.

Ryan picked me up at Crunch Gym, where I was red-faced after a twenty-minute walk on the treadmill (jealous?). We went out for coffee, then drinks, and then I took him back to my dorm room and we made out to Aimee Mann.

Ryan was a really good-looking guy in a potato bisque kind of way—he had blue eyes like turquoise jewelry and creamy, starchy skin. But he was a lousy kisser in the worst of both worlds: sloppy, *and* a pecker. Maybe it was because he was one of those handsome guys who aren't great in bed because they don't need to try hard. So, in the interest of salvaging our make-out experience, and because I've never considered myself cute enough to be able to "just lie there," I started talking dirty, narrating the action and its potential. He got excited, and it was better. We fooled around for a little while longer; my butt nestled between the writing surface and the built-in corkboard of my dorm-furniture desk. Later that evening, I walked Ryan downstairs, signed him out with the NYU security guard, and he went home to sleep underneath a table that doubled as a playing field for horizontally shiftable wooden players grafted onto steel handles able to flip completely.

LATER THAT night, I got a phone call. I squinted out my eye crunk to see the clock radio staring a red "4:45" back at me and picked up quickly, before my roommate woke up too. It was Ryan, and he was breathing deeply.

Here is me: [groggy, croaky] "Hello?"

"Hi," said the random guy I met at the gym, in a tiny, faltering, intense voice; timid and urgent at once.

I was actually scared. I never heard him speak in that voice. What if he had a split personality and I was on the phone with "Stabby" Ryan? As frequent as my interactions with the mentally ill are, I still react with fear at the moment they reveal their characteristic abnormal behavior. I got scared immediately because now I knew Ryan wasn't just weird—Ryan was crazy. I could hear it in his voice. And he was calling me in the middle of the night. Hoping that he was the harmless kind of crazy, I tried to pretend on the phone that I didn't know Ryan was nuts.

Me, Again: [cranky, squawky] "Ryan, is that you?"

Ryan: "Yeah."

I waited for whatever a sane person would give as a reason why he was calling me in the middle of the night. When that didn't come, I said instead: "All right. Well, hi. What's up?"

There was a pause here, and some whimpering, like he was trying to get himself to say what he'd called to say, shy around his intentions. Like what you hear when a dog is making the decision to do something he's not supposed to, but really wants to do, like steal a scrap from the kitchen counter or drop the sock in its mouth to howl at a high-pitched sound. From his urgency and his hemming, it seemed like Ryan had been thinking about what he wanted to say since he left my dorm.

He continued, in his itsy voice. "I'm just . . . I'm just up, and I'm thinking about you, and . . . and . . ."

"Yeah?" I prompted, impatient and vocally beginning to sound a little like Joy Behar, which is what happens when Jewish girls decide they have no more patience. He could have said anything at that point. "I want to be a tiger." "You smell like German Potato Salad." "Let's rob a train." He was a crazy person. It didn't have to make sense. I just wanted him to be out with it.

"Well," Ryan continued, "I was thinking about what I wanna do with you."

Oh, there it was. Ryan was calling about sex. That was the emergency. I'd started something with our ribald discourse earlier in the night, and now his erotic expression was flowing. I wished he'd figured out what he'd wanted to say earlier in the evening, when I was sitting on the desk, his tongue wedged in my ear like a slab of clay. Now he was creeping me out and it was 4:50 a.m., and there was still a good chance he could say something bonkers about how his mom is made of celery or that he wanted to wear my neck skin as an ascot.

"Uh-huh," I coaxed, less Behar-like, but still wary.

"Well," Ryan said. "I've been thinking, like I said, about what I want, and. And . . . well. Here's the thing." He inhaled deeply. Then, he continued.

"I really want to share a cock with you."

Here is where the long pause goes, and a couple of rapid eye blinks until I'm super-awake, and then, now, also, the disappointing music they use on *The Price Is Right* when a contestant overbids on the Showcase Showdown or puts the disk in the wrong slot on the Plinko board or otherwise screws up her chances of winning a prize. *Bom-bom-ba-WOOOOOOO.*

"What?" I asked, which is the only way to respond to what was said.

"I want to share a cock with you," Ryan repeated. "I want to have a three-way with you and another guy. So badly."

So, that was it? He'd had a sexual epiphany in the middle of the night, and suddenly it was my responsibility to vet his fantasy, just because I had him over and unleashed the beast when I started yammering? It was at once the most artless and poorly timed request for a three-way I'd ever borne witness to, but at the same time, a huge relief. Now that I knew why he was calling, the odds were considerably diminished that Ryan was outside my dorm with a crème brûlée torch and a hacksaw. He was just awake, and pleading me for a cock-share, or at least an ear to lend.

NOW, I'VE thought about having three-ways before, because I'm an *American.* But there's a wide gulf of difference between thinking about something that *seems* like a hoot and actually going through the steps to make it happen. For example, I used to joke about how "fun" it would be to drop acid and see Rosie O'Donnell play the Cat in the Hat in *Seussical*, when it was still on Broadway. Sure, it *seems* like it would be hilarious, but once you're in the Richard Rodgers Theatre, and your armrests are melting, and Horton is singing a ballad about how nobody understands him, all of a sudden it's not so funny anymore.

But Ryan wasn't joking, and I needed a moment to sort out his request. I'd never dated a guy who wanted a three-way with a "guy-guy-girl" ratio, which, admittedly, holds the most appeal to me, of all possible permutations. Being the only girl seems like an awful lot of attention, and I was used to feeling like I did backflips for the interest of the one attractive guy who came around every second solstice. The bounty of two erections seemed decadent. I imagine I'd feel like a starving refugee at the hot bar at Whole Foods, except the steaming curried chicken would be rubbing its groin against my butt and the garlic potatoes would be slapping its balls against my chin. It's still more appealing to me than the popular alternative. I've always taken offense to the "girl-girl-guy" arrangement, because, with the exception of maybe Oskar Schindler, I don't believe there's a man who's ever lived who has deserved sex with more than one woman at a time. I don't mean to disparage men: I'm just saying they're way more advantaged than women in pretty much every department, but especially when it comes to having their pick of great girls. Do they really need two of us at a time? Isn't it enough that they "run society"? A guy claiming he's entitled to a three-way with two women is like a chubby kid demanding frosting on his Snickers bar.

It was also Ryan's phrasing that turned me off. He didn't want to share me. "Me" was not the object of his sentence.

He wanted to share an as-yet-unprocured cock. Besides being alerted to what may be generously described as Ryan's bi-curiosity—and sure, to this day, Nate and I still refer to him by his nickname, "Ry-curious"—I think it was the concept of sharing itself that turned me off most of all.

Because what's the point of going guy-guy-girl if you're not the star of the show? Fuck sharing. I live alone, I don't have any sisters, and I grew up the younger of two, my older brother a substantial eight years my senior, which afforded him "third parent" status in our household. I don't like sharing anything, including clothes, sandwiches, and attention. I relate to Daffy Duck's "mine mine mine all mine" policy. And also, I mean, please; like anybody's cock is so big that you'd be like, "I can't finish this! Let's split it."

Also, as I mentioned, there was the bi thing. Bi doesn't always mean gay, but when I hear it from men, I take it to mean "gay soon." It's like when you meet an anorexic who's still eating ice cubes. So when I got Ryan's phone call, and he said what he said, I thought to myself right away, "Wow, that's pretty gay" and, also, "This is over."

Nobody loves gay guys more than me. But you can't date them, and even Liza has learned by now that you can't marry them, even if they love you so much they can let themselves forget that you have a vagina. They never forget that you have boobs—everybody likes those, and they're fun to put in rhinestone dresses. But closeted gays who end up turning their hags into beards are capable of confusing themselves to the point of becoming temporarily blinded to their true orientation, in the name of loving everything about a woman except for the hole between her legs. (The other one.) But straight girls deserve to be with men who can't stop thinking about pussy, even when they are giving a eulogy or changing a diaper. And gay guys can't give us that.

It's a double standard, because a little bit of bi in a boy turns the boy gay. But even a heap of bi in a girl can still mean you're just dealing with a straight woman who happens to be super horny. It's not the same. And while plenty of girls are open-minded when it comes to kissing their boyfriends in "grunge drag" lipstick, I don't think that even comes close to getting turned on seeing your beloved with a dick in his mouth.

Ryan was hardly my beloved at that point; he was just some random cutie I was getting to know. And I guess there's something shitty about being so knee-jerk in my ideas about what makes a suitable male partner. After all, isn't the idea of a guy getting fucked only degrading because it makes him more like a woman?

Maybe that was just it. I didn't want to date a bisexual guy any more than I wanted to date a woman. And I don't want to date women. The closest I ever came to hooking up with a girl is when I went over to Regina Mancini's apartment to smoke pot and order Chinese food, and ended up feeling her boobs because Vivian, the girl she had a crush on, didn't show up. I played makeshift second fiddle to absentee Vivian, getting bossed around by Regina, a petite Sicilian who would go on to become a traffic cop. It wasn't hot. I played with Regina's tits with benign curiosity, like a child fooling around with pizza dough or Flubber. I played with them the way gay guys feel up their prom dates.

I POLITELY got off the phone with Ryan the night of his confession, explaining that I had to get up for a History of Television class in a mere fourteen hours, and soon after that, we went our separate ways. I imagine he figured out that we were not what either of us wanted, and I hope he found what he did.

I ran into Ryan five years later, in the Carroll Gardens neighborhood of Brooklyn where my then-boyfriend lived at the time. Ryan was sitting next to a pretty girl—another redhead, as a matter of fact—on the same side of a booth at a burrito place on Smith Street. I said hello and introduced my boyfriend, and everybody was very nice, making mannered chitchat in what would have otherwise been an awkward interaction. My boyfriend and I left with our take-out, and I couldn't help looking back over my shoulder to see if Ryan and his new girlfriend were joined, after our departure, by a third party, maybe returning from the men's room to sit across from them in the booth. That wasn't the case, but I did notice they were sharing a burrito. Good for them.

white noise

There are two major things you need to know about Colin. The first is that he was the frontman of what was at the time considered a very important noise band. The second is that he loved the taste of his own semen.

Colin and I spent a lot of time talking on the phone when I was a sophomore in college, at first because I was interviewing him for a school magazine, and then because I had a big fat crush on the guy. Colin was forty-one to my nineteen, which paralleled our physical distance. He lived in Northern California, and I was in New York. We spoke on the phone frequently during what, today, I can assuredly dub the loneliest period of my adult life. I hadn't met Nate yet, I was starting to grow apart from Ronit, whom I'd remained friends with since Hebrew school, and the only person in my life besides "punk rock enough to eat food out of the garbage" Eve was my roommate

Jodi, she of the missing row of knuckles, a hand deformity I never got used to. Jodi played the first two Ben Folds Five albums around our dorm constantly, and I blame that music for permeating what was already a melancholy, twee sort of "Billy Joel meets *Pippin* with a yeast infection" period of my life. I'd listen to Colin's band to cut the aftertaste from all that cascading, piano-y Chapel Hill pop. His music was alienating, clever, and practically unlistenable; Colin's albums were castaways in my CD collection, left over from high school.

But this isn't a story about music. This is a story about how I was so lonely that I spoke every-other-nightly on the phone with an eccentric string bean who got so excited about whatever he happened to be talking about—politics, music, art— that he would end up lecturing me on subjects for hours. I couldn't tell if Colin was brilliant or even smart; he made sense, so he wasn't totally bananas. But enthusiasm and loquaciousness can be a decent guise for what is otherwise a mediocre intellect. I couldn't tell. I was just so glad to be on the phone with a guy I thought was kind of interesting, who made music that I'd listened to in high school. It's a popular fantasy to get with a guy you used to think was attractive from afar, and at the very least, talking to Colin distracted me from the millionth repetition of "Selfless, Cold and Composed" that blasted from Jodi's room, ten feet away.

My "conversations" with Colin would have been more two-sided if I were taking notes: our relationship was an accidental correspondence course in Colin 101. He'd get himself worked up about some abstract concept rooted in the discipline of new media or transcendental meditation or why it's wrong to advertise junk food to children, and the next thing I'd know, I'd be peeing into the plastic Bed, Bath & Beyond wastebasket I kept in my bedroom instead of interrupting him to ask whether I could call him back after I used the bathroom.

I understand if you need to go back and reread that last part. But indeed, peeing in the garbage can is what I did—on more than one occasion—because I would feel self-conscious stopping Colin in the middle of his impressive flow of enthusiastic discourse in order to start a flow of my own. It's out of character for me not to use a toilet like a civilized person with no desire to mark one's territory or to save one's body fluids in the name of eccentricity, agoraphobia, or sloth. But I didn't want the flush to gross out Colin (though apparently I have no qualms disgusting *you*), and I couldn't just leave my urine in the tank for Jodi to find later. No, clearly the best and most socially considerate thing to do in deference to my long-distance professor/imaginary boyfriend and my disfiguredly digited roommate was to piss in a garbage can, wipe myself with Kleenex, then pour the fluid waste down the communal bathtub—a relatively silent endeavor.

I told you this was a dark period of my life.

So, even though I didn't feel technically necessary when I was on the phone with Colin, he still figured that it would be a good idea to buy himself a plane ticket to come out and visit me for a weekend. I don't know why he felt compelled to meet me, honestly. Short of a dial tone, I was the most passive phone audience I can imagine. But maybe that's what appealed to him about me. Plus, my fandom, my age. My vagina. No, I'm not bragging—I had one, even then.

So, Colin came out to visit. And I remember being attracted to him right away. He was tall and thin, with salt-and-pepper hair, and tattoos all over his arms. He dressed like a kid, in jeans and T-shirts and sneakers, as all musicians do, whether they're forty-one or sixteen. And in person, he was similarly gregarious, geeky, and oddly indifferent to my presence. Until we fucked each other.

It was tough to get through to Colin, even once he got to New York, that my principle interest in him was romantic. I think guys like him are preternaturally oblivious to connections beyond the pale of the casual. It's a musician thing, I think. Those guys are just happy to make friends, and they seem to have a bevy of different kinds of relationships across the country. All those amicable connections prove resourceful for touring because they'll always have a place to stay, whether it's with fans, peers, idols, groupies, or fellow freaks. Part of being a musician is the ability to form and release weak social bonds, if only because of the travel involved in making one's living. Then, there's the task of navigating boundaries with the fellow guys in your band: the fittest survivors in that racket tend to be the easiest-going. It's a big reason why I, Captain Intensity, am fundamentally incompatible with those of the Wah Wah Brotherhood.

But whether he'd known or not, I'd already decided, in my typically impudent, freshly adolescent fashion, that I wanted Colin to fuck me, under the covers of my twin-size dorm bed, even though one of the only things I knew about him personally—as opposed to what I knew about his music—was that he was not only a vegetarian, but he was a vegan. And Colin was one of the first vegans I'd ever met.

NOW, I am probably about to alienate the remaining six or seven young women who like Sleater-Kinney and confused this book with *The Veganomicon* just because it landed in the Alternative Women's Studies section of your locally owned independent bookstore, but I have to go on record about the following. I haven't met a lot of vegans who aren't a little crazy, a little dumb, a bit of both, or a lot of either. And I've met plenty since Colin.

I love animals, and I watch what I eat. I'm the furthest thing from Ted Nugent you can be while still loving Dolly Parton. But I think of veganism as a counterculturally sanctioned eating disorder. There are different kinds of people who go vegan for different reasons, and here's a rough working field guide.

Firstly, there are Animal Rights Vegans. These include misanthropes who prefer the company of their pets to conversations with humans, and people who *love* starting emotionally heated fights that nobody can win. Some "adopt" feral cats off the street—even the ones that will claw your face into skin ribbon—because they feel so bad for the homeless cats, they forget that they are wild animals, like crocodiles or kangaroos, which have no place inside of an apartment. Animal Rights Vegans have no problem with PETA—its objectification of women in its ad campaigns, its KKK campaign for which protestors wore white sheets outside the Westminster Dog Show to protest the "eugenics" of purebreds, or that poster they ran comparing chicken farms to concentration camps. That's how much the Animal Rights Vegan can actively dislike people.

There's also the Anti-Preservative/Hormone/Antibiotic/Chemical Vegan. This group includes paranoid, antiestablishment kids or kidults eager to blame their problems on large corporate infrastructures, as though businesses that earn more than thirty grand a year had been designed to personally destroy them. This type makes up the majority of male vegans, from my experience, especially those who interpret their preference of beer to pork as some kind of deciding vote against The Man. That's right, "The Man." Politically, The APHAC Vegan is still at the philosophical evolution of a circa-1964 Lenny Bruce, one of the most overrated stand-up comedians of all time. (Most underrated? Mo'Nique. The END.) This category of vegans includes performance artists who run for mayor as a goof, bike messengers who sprout dreadlocks from Caucasian hair by not washing it frequently, and people who sneer in the face of science, consistently opting out of Western medicinal revelations like antibiotics, preferring instead to treat infections with herbal tea. There are also a lot of overweight people in this category who claim they went vegan for the sake of being healthier, and there is no population on earth—including people who traverse malls with the aid of a Jazzy Scooter—who consume more cookies, fries, cake, and breads, rationalizing that it's OK, because their carbs are baked with soy butter, agave nectar, and carob chips.

Finally, there's the Anorexic Vegan, delighted to be able to blend into her surroundings by adopting a style of eating that's considered acceptable for reasons besides "I want to starve myself until I disappear and never have to deal with the time I was molested." These include women who would put restrictions on what they consider acceptable eating no matter what, and have the book *Skinny Bitch* to thank for endorsing a diet with a socially conscious veneer when, in actuality, all these girls want to do is sip hot water for dinner until they look like a corpse. There are subtler variations of these girls; the Heidi Pratt types in stilettos and minis and people in fashion who don't have a sense of humor. I met one emaciated

Los Feliz resident who told me, over the eerie silence of her still-running hybrid, that she thought it was "heroic" to avoid dairy, milk, and eggs. "Uh-huh," I said, then asked, "Do you know what *words mean*?"

SO, THOSE are some vegans I've met. And then there are the kinds of people who call themselves vegans, but eat cheese or fish on occasion, and those people are A-OK by me, one thousand percent, because those people are not vegans—they are vegetarians. And vegetarians are great, as long as they don't try to convert me while I'm tucking into a shepherd's pie, because that's very Church of Jesus Christ of Latter-day Saints, and if I wanted to talk to men who wear short sleeved shirts with neckties and who read the Bible all day, I'd go to AA.

But Colin was the first vegan I ever met, and he fit into the second category—The Anti–Preservative/Hormone/Anti-biotic/Chemical Vegan—because his eating choices very much reflected his political views, which had a lot to do with opting out of corporate culture, and other concepts that are really exciting to people going through puberty. The other thing that was distinctively immature about Colin was that he had no sense of what to say around women who wanted to sleep with him in order to keep himself, for lack of a better term, attractive to them.

"Boy, the flight out here was really long," he told me over (vegan!) fries at the Cloister Café across from my dorm. "They didn't have any meals without eggs or cheese or meat, so I brought a head of raw broccoli on the plane with me and munched on it the whole way over. I think the woman next to me was kind of grossed out by my broccoli farts after the first four hours."

And so on.

But I, in my lonely days, reacted to most of Colin's personality by plugging up my ears with my fingers and singing my favorite song: "I Can't Hear You," which I'm sure, by now, is in the public domain.

So we fooled around, and I got to watch Colin thaw into a slightly more attentive version of himself. As soon as we got physical, his monologues became conversations. The miracle of sex! It *does* help boys notice you! And my wastebasket was mercifully free of urine that whole weekend. Colin was also, incidentally, endowed with the most enormous penis I'd ever seen in my life, an appendage on behalf of which I actually had to run errands. I remember buying Magnum brand condoms at Duane Reade with a twinkle in my eye like Gene Kelly's while he splashed in the puddles outside Debbie Reynolds's house.

Soon, Colin and I were telling each other what we wanted in bed, and although he was uncomfortable at first with the kind of conversation that didn't involve enlightening me about how the Australians are superior to Americans because they ban billboards in certain areas of their countryside, he slowly began to talk to me, more and more, about what he wanted to do with the baseball bat he kept in his pants.

"You know what else I imagine?" he said one night, confusing "imagine" with "request."

"I would really like it if you took my cum in your mouth when you were done going down on me, and then you let me kiss you with my tongue so I could taste my own cum."

Anybody unfortunate enough to have sat through Kevin Smith's *Clerks* (the best of what is a largely reprehensible oeuvre) will know that the sexual act Colin described is known as "snowballing." And while requesting that favor was a bit surprising, it was not something outright uncalled-for, like asking me to shit on his father's face, a variation I believe was addressed in *Jay and Silent Bob Strike Back*. And because I was having pussy-stretching sex with a guy I was really attracted to, I did it.

It's really a tribute to the female bonding hormones that are released when you're getting good-laid that you're pretty much up for anything exclusive of fisting your sister. I wondered what was *in* Colin's semen, considering his diet. Was our affair just a nefarious scheme to get me to eat tempeh?

Anyway, that happened, and he was really turned on, and then, the next time, he told me he was going to come on me and lick it off, and then he did, and soon enough, he was just eating his own semen and I was there as a witness.

I felt like I did on the phone—unnecessary. I mean, what's the point of having a girl in the room if all you want to do is dine on your own jizz? Why not cut out the middleman?

Colin was probably just starving for animal protein, poor guy. No wonder he was obsessed. It's like how all dieters do is think about cupcakes, or how all Catholics do all day is imagine how much fun it would be to get an abortion.

COLIN SOON returned to whence he came—to his recording studio and his band and his ideas and his touring schedule. He called me a couple of times after that weekend, but our conversations went back to the way they were before. I was superfluous—an appendage, and not as formidable as the one between his gawky legs. He told me how much he wanted to drop acid with me in the desert, and how much he hated New York City; two things that pretty much make me as dry as a "Shouts &

Murmurs" column. Soon enough, we went our separate ways. Me with the knowledge that our differences were insurmountable, and him knowing, wherever he is—probably Portland—that somebody once witnessed him feasting on the kind of intimate delicacy that is not technically permissible on a vegan diet.

turn down the glamour

During my last year at college, I decided to open my horizons, which is a fancy word for "legs." I figured that if I was less picky about the guys I hooked up with—as though that was ever my problem—I'd increase my odds of finding somebody good. It is not an absurd philosophy by any means, as long as you're not too emotional about it.

I tried dating boys from school for once: a pockmarked, handsome weirdo with Clark Kent glasses from my photography seminar; a schlubby, Jewish tall guy who lived in the dorm room next to mine who blathered on about De La Soul before asking me if he could use my bathroom, then taking an extraordinary crap in the toilet that was, ostensibly, right next door to his own. And then there was Jazz Matt, Nate's nickname for the skinny Daniel Stern lookalike from my screenwriting class who interned at Small's Jazz Club because he *looooooved*

Jazz. Jazz Matt's real name was just regular Matt, but Nate and I came up with the bright idea to call him "Jazz Matt" because it rhymes with "Jazz Cat." And few things were funnier to us than the idea of Matt "jazzing-out" to cool-be-boo-bebop-scat-a-tat-tastic, heroin-ific jazz, when in fact he was just this geeky white jerk who, given a chance, would like nothing more than to sit quietly in a room, sipping tea.

Jazz Matt fizzled out during our pitiful Gil-Scott-Heron-fueled make-out session, so he couldn't throw his jazz hat into the ring for the boyfriend position I was interviewing intensively for. But something was coming together for me around this time that was new. I didn't sweat J-Matt, and I didn't stalk or fume once my crush had petered out its torque. Maybe my hormones had finally learned to shut the hell up for a minute, or maybe I'd shed some of the ego-fueled "how dare *he* not love *me*" vitriol that was conjoined like an evil twin to the star-crossed circumstances of every guy that didn't come through. Either way, around that time, I began to get a little better at letting go. And there were plenty of guys around whom I walked away from before they even had time to express interest—the defecating neighbor comes to mind.

Then, right before I turned twenty-one, I met my first real boyfriend.

DAVID WAS just a year older than me, and his intelligence was visible from across the room. He was a particular kind of quiet, and there are different kinds—there's shy/socially phobic quiet, angry and plotting quiet, blissful Zen quiet, illiterate farmhand quiet. David's quiet was patient and smart—the kind you need to get through a ton of books. I wondered if I seemed too frivolous for him; I had pink leopard prints pasted all over my dorm room walls, and Spice Girls posters hanging alongside framed photos of John Waters.

But David liked me, and soon enough we got together. I loved falling in love. I loved the whole incubation period: all the lazing about in bed staring into each other's faces, the midsummer hangouts on his fire escape, the activity of the night being listening to a record or taking a walk. I was having the time of my life being loved as what I gleaned was an adult. I would say to people, "I have a *boyfriend*. This is my *boyfriend*." And after my mint-condom-sucking, Jazz Matt–chasing college days, I was ripe and delighted in the sensation of being courted in a proper way, by a boy who didn't just think I was sexy. David thought I was adorable.

We went to Montauk together. We drank Mike's Hard Lemonade in a motel room and read *Penthouse* to each other in the rental car back to the city. I let him take my picture without any makeup, on the beach. Around David, I felt cherubic and endearing.

It didn't work out.

There were differences—the kind that have nothing to do with him liking that band the Mountain Goats when you feel like hearing that guy's singing voice is like being stabbed in the eye with a shrimp fork over and over again. He loved me, but I also think he was infatuated with somebody in me I wasn't so crazy about. If Nate was the one who saw Kate Pierson underneath my grubby disaffect when we met, David tried to strip away all of Kate's lovely lashes and wigs and iridescent outfits to reveal what he was confident was the mousy, wide-eyed ragamuffin little girl that he wanted to love me as, and who he wanted me to be. It would come out in little things, like how he told me how pretty I looked in a T-shirt when I let my hair go into its natural wave, or in acts of faith in my talent, like when we'd try to collaborate and he'd write me a part that was more in his voice than mine.

After we split, David went on to reach his goal of becoming a successful television comedy writer, which was never a surprise given his talent and work ethic, and one day, I came into his office to interview for an on-air/writing position on the show he worked on. After the meeting, I stopped by his desk to say hello.

I wore what I always wear to interviews: a suit, with heels and makeup. I did not wear a ball gown and a beehive.

David asked how my meeting with his boss went, then did that thing he always does where he smiles and cringes at the same time. It's sweet, but it also makes you feel a little awkward, so you're compelled to counter it with false stoicism or cool. And when the neurotic Jew is the cool one, well.

Then David lowered his voice a bit. "Let me give you a bit of advice," he told me, on his turf. And I listened for his tip because I wanted that job.

"When you're around an office like this one," he continued, "Well . . . you might want to turn down the glamour."

I can't pile on when it comes to David. He was a great boyfriend at a time when I needed a great boyfriend more than anything, and *I* broke up with *him*, then displayed a novice's ignorance when insisting that we still be friends, unaware of the rule that the person who initiates a breakup has no say about what the relationship then becomes.

But that advice coming from him to "turn down the glamour" gave me a bedrock *Legally Blonde* moment that propelled me into sweet, revenge-fueled action. It is what has motivated me to succeed in my field. Because as frequently or insistently as nerdy, quiet guys may claim that they are outcasts, the reality is that once high school is over, they are the ones who get the jobs. And those jobs include but are not limited to writing for television, art direction, graphic design, songwriting, blogging, video editing, copywriting, filmmaking, working for public radio, and so on and so on, and whatever job you do can probably go here too. Right now, in the places where I live and work and date, the timid, geeky guy prevails. And the only way to pass in their world if you're a girl is to play the game and blend into the herd. David illuminated something about the way things are that made me furious, despite what his intentions were when he gave me his two cents. And no, I didn't get that job.

What I have since learned is that the girls who thrive in Boytown, professionally and personally, are the mousy ones. The ones who don't know how to walk in heels or do their own eyeliner. The girls who don't know how to play hostess to a good party or that they need to write a thank-you note and bring a gift when visiting someone's home. They wear their "nice" New Balance sneakers when they go out at night, and a clean T-shirt when they go to work. They blend in with the guys they scare; the ones who hate them for not chasing them in high school.

"You wear too much makeup," David would tell me when we were together. Like I had any business taking advice from a guy who'd wear a T-shirt with a Chinese-food restaurant menu printed on it to a dinner date. You can't throw the first stone when you dole out what you assume are compliments, but what is really just backhanded armchair criticism from somebody looking to create the ideal girl.

★　　★　　★

I'M FASCINATED by what men think is the perfect woman. Cameron Diaz in *There's Something About Mary* is just one of many man-made dream girls. Remember? Mary was a sports surgeon, a beer-swilling football enthusiast, and a golfer, but she was also feminine, leggy, lithe, and blond, with a bottomless well of compassion for her retarded brother. She was basically a guy with a woman's big heart, wrapped up in a "tight little package." She wasn't funny, but she had a great laugh, which is perfect for making funny guys feel appreciated.

Scarlett Johansson's "Cristina," in *Vicky Cristina Barcelona,* is another creature constructed in a lab by a male mind. Cristina is sprung from Woody Allen's dirty old 'mangination—a fabrication, really, of qualities attractive to him that no real girl has in one spot. Her lack of focus in tandem with her raw creative talent just crying out to be shaped by an elder. Her free-spiritedness on matters of hooking up with women, men, or both at once. Her ridiculously full lips and tits evoking Marilyn Monroe, who, even off-camera, lived—or tried to—in a fable as America's most beloved dumb slut. Marilyn was funny, too, by the way. But nobody noticed.

And then there's Pam.

The archetype of the perfect girl for guys I see all around me is, I think, best understood by taking a look at the character of Pam from NBC's *The Office.*

Pam started out on that show as a wry receptionist with a conspiratorial half-smile and wavy hair the color of milk chocolate that looks like it was wet when she left her place, and air-dried on her way to work. She's portrayed by the gorgeous and funny actress Jenna Fischer, who puts herself in the hands of makeup and wardrobe people who are responsible for making her look like less of a knockout than she is. And indeed

Pam is not supposed to be the kind of beauty that turns heads in a room.

She is bright, but not ambitious. She has a crap job, but she takes it in stride: It's good enough for Pam, for now. As a romantic pursuit, she's a slow burn: the kind of girl who will only sleep with you after months or even years of wearing down with flirty jokes and one-of-the-boys-style teasing. The men in her office—most of them—pretend she's sexually invisible. Her boss puts her down as a frump, an underdog.

Pam's equivalent from the British version of *The Office*, Dawn, was a different kind of girl entirely. Dawn was also shy, but a bit slatternly and hyperfeminine; she was always trying to be something she wasn't, quite. Her ample bust would strain the abilities of a button-down shirt, which she'd have to take in a size up or suffer cleavage. She was a little soft; like Baby-Fat Spice. Lucy Davis, who played Dawn, had those extra ten pounds of lager weight that's somehow still acceptable on beautiful television stars across the Atlantic. And, like Pam, Dawn was the romantic lead of the series.

Both could land a joke. Both could melt the camera with a small smile. But Pam is bland, unassuming; faded wallpaper. And Dawn was a coquette in corporate casual. If Dawn was Ginger, Pam was Mary-Ann's *cousin*—the one who can't even get her hair into pigtails, so she just lets it hang.

I've met a lot of guys my age who have crushes on Pam that are so intense, it says more about what they want than who this character is supposed to be. They don't just like her; they relate to her. They're underdogs too. And what they want is who they are.

Pam is not intimidating, like one of those women who

wears makeup and tailored clothes, and has a good job that she enjoys, and confidence, and an adult woman's sexuality. There's nothing scary about Pam, because there's no mystery: she's just like the boys who like her; mousy and shy. The ultimate emo-boy fantasy is to meet a nerdy, cute girl just like him, and *nobody else will realize she's pretty*. And she'll melt when she sees his re-cord collection because it's just like hers, and she'll swoon when he plays her the song he wrote on the guitar, and she'll never want to go out to a party for which he'll be forced to comb his hair, or buy grown-up shoes or tie a tie, or demonstrate a hearty handshake, or make eye contact, or relate to people who work in different fields, or to basically act like a man.

Remember when men and women could be different, though? And women being different wasn't a burden, but sort of a turn-on? Because really, men and women aren't *that* differ-ent. One likes astrology more than car chases for some reason, but we're ultimately all looking for the same thing—to be loved and understood. We're all insecure; we're all imperfect and we have the empathy that makes us try not to be too mean to one another. We all like being respected and challenged and having fun and eating delicious snacks. But to some guys, the ways girls are different than boys is the beast under the bed; the pussy with teeth. The horrors of having to make conversation with a woman who's never seen *Transformers* or doesn't care how the Knicks are doing this season is the stuff of their nightmares. It's like they just want themselves with a vagina.

The trick is to realize that the boys who talk so much about being rejected that it seems like they're proud of it aren't neces-sarily sweeter or more sensitive than the Bababooey-spouting frat bullies who line up at clubs like SkyBar to run game on girls they want to date rape. There are plenty of nerds who fear women and *aren't* sensitive, despite their marketing; they just dislike women in a new, exciting way. Timid racists aren't "sensitive" because they lock their car doors when they see a black person on the street. They're just too scared to get out of the car and shout the "N" word.

Fear can be the result of admiration, or it can be a symptom of contempt. When I see squeamish guys passing over qualified women when they're hiring for a job, or becoming tongue-tied when a girl crashes their all-boy conversation at a party, I don't credit them for being awestruck. They're reacting to the intimidating female as an intruder, an alien, and somebody they can't relate to. It's not a compliment to be made invisible.

star wars is a kids' movie

Rob was the kind of guy who'd come on like a roll of Charmin Ultra when you were unavailable; strong and sensitive, dripping with Aloe lotion. Then, once you'd cleared your heart's calendar for his penis, he'd be wadded up in the corner, stuck to the medicine cabinet, sopping with tears and of no use to anyone.

When Rob and I met, I was seeing somebody else, which didn't faze him a bit. He was an actor, so his area of expertise was believing he was awesome and working hard to charm people into thinking so too. So when we met, and he decided he wanted me, flirty e-mails flowed out of him like taffy from the business end of a wide-gauge candy pipe; cloying and consistent. When we'd get together, he'd use my name in conversation a lot, a successful manipulation technique for narcissists like me who are easily hypnotized by the sound of their own names. And it worked.

"Let's get dinner, Julie."

Duh, OK.

We went to a glorified diner called Bendix, and it wasn't a date, because I had a boyfriend. Rob wasn't initially attractive to me, but because he was so gooey and determined, I grew fond of him quickly. I think there's something beyond the grass being greener that fuels one's attraction to men who exist outside of a relationship you're in. It permits you to twist the reality of meeting what's merely a self-centered guy who wants what he can't have into a self-congratulatory progress tale. You think to yourself, "Well, I'm different *now*—I'm *girlfriend material*—so, of course he wants to be with me. If only I weren't in this dumb relationship with a guy who's already proven he wants to be my boyfriend, I'd be in the throes of what is an oyster-like world of pearl-paved streets. Dumb Guy Who Loves Me! Doesn't he realize how explosively the universe has changed since I've been cooped up being loved within the confines of reality?"

After Bendix, and its ensuing meatloaf, Rob walked me home and kissed me. And as soon as he did, I felt every last cell in my body rush with guilt. I am too inherently neurotic to ever cheat on somebody without treating myself to a concurrent crucifixion, so the day after I was kissed, I broke it off with the guy I was dating so I could begin to legitimately fall for Rob. I was positive that he, liberal gusher of my own name during seduction, was a sure thing. I couldn't wait to tell Rob I was newly single; he was going to pounce on me like I was a Beggin' Strip.

Hahahaha! When people are wrong, it's funny.

MY ON-THE-MARKETNESS was like an unsolicited homework assignment for the guy who, twenty-four-hours earlier, was falling over himself to charm me with compliments lavished over too-expensive loaves of meat. I saw his behavior flip a bitch. Clearly, Rob was freaked out that I'd actually gone through with the steps I had to take in order to date him with a clear conscience, and now he felt responsible for my being available.

After that, we would get together for what I suppose are technically dates to a twenty-two-year-old, which is how old I was at the time, but since he was thirty-one, I can't really call what we were doing "dating." We were hanging out and hooking up, which is what girls in their twenties expect and men at any age want, because it preserves the ambiguity of an affair and absolves guys from any responsibility when somebody gets hurt. By the time the sex began, we weren't on a level playing field.

After we started sleeping together, I began showing red flag signs of wanting not just sex but all its trimmings (intimacy, brunch, etc), and Rob started showing more and more signs of "Get Out of My Roomism." That's what I call the disease that comes from the boyhood instinct to yell at one's little sister when she gets her chocolaty fingers on a rare issue of *MAD* magazine, or at one's mom when she wants to use the bathroom and you're still in the tub, playing with yourself. It's only when a guy passes thirty and still wants girls to leave him alone and stay away from his stuff does that behavior become disconcerting.

When Rob and I were hooking up, we would always sleep at my apartment. He was superprotective of his space, and also, as it turned out, paranoid about being seen with me around his friends, because, he explained, he was concerned they would "gossip." That's a double-threat of sorry-ass. It was quickly becoming clear, even to a self-congratulatory progress tale in her early twenties, that there was no fucking way in the world Rob wanted to be my boyfriend. He'd invite me to see one of his shows, then he'd have me meet him a block away once he got offstage, so nobody would see us leaving the theater together and speculate that we were an item. It wasn't because he was cheating on anybody; he was just sort of a dick.

I'd never had the experience of being anyone's *secret lover*— the girl who hides in the garbage can or shows up wearing a false mustache. "Dating" Rob was the closest I'd come to being with a guy who cared more about what his friends thought than how the girl he was screwing felt. I didn't get that at all. Why didn't he just fuck his friends? If he was that concerned about what they thought, they must be pretty great!

I chewed him out over that "wait for me around the corner" bullroar, because even with the self-esteem of a twenty-two-year-old, I was never a doormat. I told him that he was pushing me away, and what the fuck was that when paired with intense sex, and also, why hadn't I been to his apartment yet? It had been a couple of months already—what was he hiding? I didn't know that this is just how some guys are, and that you should avoid them, like people with tattoos on their faces or relatives who want to borrow money. I just couldn't reconcile the way Rob was with the way he changed after I no longer had a boyfriend.

Then 9/11 happened.

HEY, DON'T you love memoirs? What other genre can footnote an unprecedented historical atrocity as a plot point in a fuck-buddy story?

"He made me wait for him around the corner, the asshole!

Then planes hit buildings and people died just because they came to work that day, and it smelled like burning tires below Fourteenth Street for a month and people who believed in God all of a sudden had to defend their certainty after bearing witness to something so uniquely senseless and chaotic and cruel. I mean, yeesh! I can't decide who's a bigger jerk—Khalid Sheikh Mohammed or that prick I was dating!"

Anyway, I remember being uncertain whether to call Rob that day. Like everybody else who lived in the city, I was getting concerned e-mails and phone calls from everybody I knew, and I remember being unsure if it was OK to get in touch with the guy I was sleeping with, or whether that wasn't too *forward*. As in, maybe, if I wasn't casual enough, he'd make me wait for him *two* blocks away next time. That was the ridiculous garbage that ricocheted around my head on 9/11, in addition to, let's just say, more universal concerns, like whether we were all going to die.

This is the compromise I made about contacting Rob during what I decided, because I am *Einstein*, was an unusual circumstance. I sent him an e-mail message with the subject header "ARE YOU OKAY?!?!?!?" in all caps, and liberally alternated question marks and exclamation points after the phrase. There was nothing in the body of the text. That kept me *mysterious*. I sent that message off to Rob and patted myself on the back. I thought my e-mail was a great balance between concern about whether or not my friend with benefits was all right after a terrorist attack, and nonchalance, which I figured would, one day, make him treat me better. Among the unfathomable multitude of things I did not know at the time is that a "friend with benefits" is like a unicorn that shits cupcakes—fun to imagine, but not actually real.

I didn't hear back from Rob that day, but in the wake of all the soot and emotional debris of, um, 9/11, I did manage to get him to invite me over to his apartment. It turns out that Rob felt vulnerable enough, by then, to extend an invitation for me to come over. So maybe the attacks were worth it! *Right, ladies?*

ROB LIVED alone, in a Brooklyn brownstone apartment I assumed his wealthy parents had bought for him. He answered the door dressed more casually than I'd seen him when we went out together, and I was put off by the draping of his athletic gray T-shirt over peg-legged mom jeans that seemed to accent what I only then noticed were his substantial, womanly hips.

I brought my friend's copy of the *Yellow Submarine* DVD, which he told me he wanted to watch when I finally got him to invite me over. The DVD was like my Golden Ticket, granting me entry into the cluttered grotto he'd kept secret for so long. Now I'd finally gained admission into the apartment of the man who'd been putting his dick in me for three months. I felt so lucky.

His place was dingy with no evidence of a woman's touch, but it wasn't filthy, nor did it seem to house an arsenal of treasures, like it seemed it should, the way he'd protected it from my eyes. When I glanced around his living room, Rob got suspicious and quiet, visibly anxious that here I was, in his territory. I have a habit of nosing around people's media when I'm in their apartments, and I browsed Rob's VHS tapes—many of them homemade and labeled *Star Wars*, while he used the bathroom. When he came out, he had a hard time making eye contact, and then he took a deep breath, like he was about to tell me something important he'd rehearsed in the bathroom before the flush.

"Listen, I don't usually have people come over here," Rob said.

"OK," I said.

"So," he continued, "could you please not look at my stuff while I'm in the bathroom?"

I told him "sure," and then took a seat on the couch and tried to stare only straight ahead of me. This guy really was the worst.

Rob put in the DVD, and, as hard as it may be to believe, I did not concentrate on the plot of *Yellow Submarine*. Instead, I marinated in my incredulity at Rob's behavior and wondered if he was hiding anything more illicit than what I'd seen on that video shelf. Were there surveillance videos? Films of women crushing baby animals with stiletto heels? Were those VHS tapes labeled in code? Because based on the amount of other *Star Wars* paraphernalia in Rob's apartment, I had a feeling that "*Star Wars*" was code for "*Star Wars*." I was in a No Girls Allowed tree house with a little boy who, despite his proclivities for Chewbacca-themed entertainment, still expected to get laid. And I was the one who'd schlepped out there after a long struggle of getting him to let me come over. It was, in fact, the only time in my life I can remember practically begging to come to Brooklyn.

By the way, I've never seen any of the *Star Wars* movies. Mostly because I think it's funny that I haven't, and also, because I've never had any interest in those films, and now it's too late. It's a children's movie, and I'm over thirty. I've also never seen the *Snorks* movie, and while I'm sure it would've helped to shape my pop culture worldview if I'd been exposed to it

earlier, today there are more pressing things on my agenda. I
also don't like sci-fi, or fantasy, or anything more *Lord of the
Rings*–ish than the Ren Faire–looking cover of that one awesome Heart record. But this George Lucas–free way of life is
totally unacceptable to guys like Rob, who was horrified—
simply *horrified*—that I hadn't seen what seemed to—still—be
his favorite movie.

Yellow Submarine ended (Spoiler alert! Ringo drowns.), and
Rob and I retired methodically to his bedroom, which housed
a dresser stuffed with more mom jeans, and a Go-Go's poster
on the wall. We started making out and I got on top of him and
stared at Belinda Carlisle's soft, pretty-dykey tan face while I al-
truistically gyrated until completion, then slept through Rob's
snores under flannel sheets that smelled like teenage boy. I let
myself out in the morning.

As poorly as our "relationship" was going, it's important to
mention that sex with Rob, despite the giant chasm between
what each of us wanted from each other, was fantastic. It is im-
possible to overstate how physically compatible we were and,
what's more, I think I was hungry to be fucked well and treated
badly by somebody I was illogically certain I wanted to one
day be my husband.

That's the other thing. Rob was the first Jewish guy I'd
ever dated, and my brain activated a subconscious launch sequence when I finally started sleeping with somebody who
seemed, in the abstract, to be at least culturally compatible. I
can only relate it to women in their late thirties who see a
baby, and they get like me when I see a Cadbury Creme Egg.
Part of what was so attractive about Rob came from some ancient instinct in my Solomon Schechter–educated, Jappy lizard
brain screeching, "Marry him! Get moneyed in-laws! Wait by

the Dumpster until you get a ring if you have to! Sue him for everything when he leaves you for a blonde!"

Soon after our Brooklyn sleepover, I got fired from my secretary job at a theater PR firm, which was a horrible gig at an office staffed by the only gay men I've ever met in my life who truly hated me. They let me go after I fucked up the setting on the Xerox machine, making too-dark copies of a press photo of Nathan Lane and Matthew Broderick, hats to hearts, heroically singing "God Bless America" during a curtain call of a *Producers* performance on September 12, 2001, captioned, "The Show Must Go On." I was relieved I didn't have to work there anymore, but also panicked and bottomless: Within the course of three weeks, I'd become unemployed and lost a boyfriend, and every night brought with it another nightmare about being on a plane on fire, about to careen into a skyscraper.

Then I found a bump on my upper lip.

MY DERMATOLOGIST at the time, an octogenarian Orthodox Jew who has since dropped dead from old age, was a gentle patriarch who would take a metal instrument to my cheek when I needed an acne breakout tamed. When I came into his office with the bump on my lip, I was certain I had an acne cyst—the kind I get on my chin sometimes. I figured getting a shot from Dr. Stanley Nussbaum's magic cortisone needle in his billion-year-old office on East Thirty-sixth Street would be a brief distraction to break up my day of looking for a new secretary job on Craigslist and obsessing over the loser I was sleeping with—but in *his bed* now!

And that's when Dr. Nussbaum told me I had herpes.

Well, actually, what he told me was that I had a cold sore. And that was insane to me, because it didn't look like a sore—it looked like a bump. And when I asked him what the difference between a cold sore and herpes was, he said, "Nothing." So when I freaked out and asked him "Are you telling me I have herpes?" he told me calmly that babies get cold sores and chicken pox is also herpes, but all I could think about was that fucking guy in his dumb bed, and how that idiot gave me a fucking STD while Jane Wiedlin helplessly watched the whole thing from her postered perch. And I was. So. Pissed. Off.

Dr. Nussbaum tried his best to calm me down, explaining at least four times that the only thing he could do was swab it and test to see whether it was the first time I'd been exposed, in which case it would be conclusive that I'd gotten it from Rob.

"I advise you to contact your boyfriend," he told me in monotone, fingering the bump with his latex gloved fingers.

"HE'S NOT EVEN MY BOYFRIEND!" I wailed to an elderly Jew with patients who needed moles biopsied waiting for him in the lobby.

After my appointment, I called Dr. Nussbaum obsessively to get my test results, even though he wouldn't answer his phone on what was then Yom Kippur. But I didn't need to know the swab results to know that I'd gotten that cold sore from Rob. Finally, the doctor called me back, and it looked like I was right. This was my first exposure, and that schmuck I'd dumped my boyfriend to date had given me a cold sore. I was "lucky" it was the mouth kind, and not the south kind.

This time, I didn't play it all "9/11 coy" with Rob. I didn't send him a blank e-mail with an all-caps header ("YOU GAVE ME HERPES?!?!"), hoping he'd think I was a cool cuke. After I calmed down, I called Rob and told him exactly what had happened. What my doctor said, how he swore to me it was no big deal, how there was an excellent chance that I'd never see a cold sore again—which I haven't—and how it looked like I got it from him. Rob called me late at night, after work at his new job. He was livid, hysterical, and accusatory.

He went to a doctor of his own soon after that, like he was retaining the services of a divorce lawyer, and called me a couple of days later. It was the most I'd ever heard from him in such a short period of time! But he wasn't calling with niceties or any kind of gentlemanly understanding that I imagine would have been greatly appreciated between sexual partners during a STD-themed crisis. "My guy said I was clean," he told me, which was gambler-speak for the news that he'd gotten a blood test that came back negative for the herpes virus, which only means that it wasn't active at the time, another myriad cold-sore-related factoid I'd learned within the course of four days in a time pre-dating my familiarity with Wikipedia. He was as paranoid and defensive as he was when I snooped his VHS tapes while he peed. Then it got worse.

"Also," he added, "I've been asking around, and I know I'm not the only guy you've been with."

What? I mean, first of all, yes. I wasn't a virgin. I'm writing this book, and what am I on, page one hundred? And I'm twenty-two? I mean, of course I'd "been with" other guys before, in the prudish manner of speaking Rob used in order to couch what was sort of a disgusting allegation. Not that we were committed to any kind of exclusivity or even formally "dating," but now that there was a cold sore and a couple of doctor bills, all of a sudden, I was the Whore of Babylon, even though since I started sleeping with Rob, I hadn't even given a second look to another guy. And before that, I was with my boyfriend, whom I hadn't strayed from, except if you count that night Rob walked me home from Bendix and planted one on my then bump-free mouth. I asked him the most appropriate question I could think of at the time.

"What the fuck do you mean you've been 'asking around'?"

Again, Rob was concerned about *gossip*, like when he worried that tongues would flap if I showed my face around the theater after his performance. Here he was again, reporting to me that people were talkin'. Who was he, Bonnie Raitt?

He told me he'd "heard" that I'd slept with one of my former improv teachers—one who'd had an on-again off-again heroin addiction. I never touched the guy. And Rob also heard that I'd slept with somebody we both knew, a writer, which was true—I totally had. But it was just once, and back when I was in college, and, like, nineteen, and we used a condom, and who cares. "And," Rob added, I'd had sex with "way more guys" than the guy I was going out with when he started hitting on me.

I pressed him for his source and did not relent, and he finally revealed the name of a girl I knew, who was friends with Nate. This girl was always icy to me and I never knew why. I assumed it was for dum-dum reasons having to do with being Nate's best hag or other bullshit girl-feud stuff I want nothing to do with. And now, apparently, she'd been talking trash about me to the guy I'd been sleeping with. And when Rob had pressed her to reveal *her* source, she had the balls to say she knew it was all true because *she'd* heard it from *Nate*.

And that's when I started hating Rob.

Hate is a lot closer to love on the emotive spectrum, and I'd officially crossed over into the "Fuck You" zone the moment Rob dropped Nate's name, as though he was trying to argue a case and revealed his surprise witness in the form of my best friend who, according to his story, "betrayed me." The hubris and ambition of that kind of ill will stunned me. Rob's talents as an actor were modest at best: being a terrible jerk was where he shone bright.

INSTANTLY, IT all came crashing down. I learned more from breaking up with Rob in that short period of time than I had in twenty-two years on the planet. Like how there's no such thing as fucking somebody good-bye. And that I apparently can't hold a "real" job at an office. And that there are a ton of boys like Rob: impudent ten-year-olds in thirtysomething clothing, which apparently can include jeans designed to fit a woman with enormous hips. That people exactly like that shit clown will happily screw you just as long as you don't touch their stuff or burden them with "grown-up problems," like herpes, or feelings. I learned that when a guy dates you for three months and you still can't call him your boyfriend, it's time to figure out why it is you're still hooking up with him. And learned that there's no time more ideal than your early twenties, when you're unemployed and haven't yet found the discipline to write, to become obsessed with a guy with no interest in catching you after you initiated a trust fall from your last relationship. I also learned that forgiveness is a slow burn.

I got around to granting amnesty to that girl who spread those rumors about me like warm peanut butter on floppy Wonder Bread. She cut off all her hair soon after Rob dumped me, which he did, after reading me that laundry list of guys I had and hadn't slept with over the phone. She apologized to me after I accidentally sat next to her at a bar, because I didn't recognize her new look, and she was pretty sincere.

"I never in my life acted like such a cunt, and I'm so sorry,"

she said, and I forgave the human being looking into my eyes.
But I still don't even make eye contact with Rob when I see
him around. Of course I'm over him, even though it took a
long time to go from hating and hurting to not caring at all.
But that experience acquainted me with the sorts of things a
spoiled man will take from you if you let him charm you into
it. And I guess, by now, I forgive him. But just like that terrible
day and all its collateral damage—I will Never Forget.

SECTION THREE

"crazy" is an std

"He would always act like he was passively a victim . . . But really he was just trying to get away with whatever he could get away with, walking all over people."

—Kathy Goodell, R. Crumb's ex-girlfriend, from *Crumb*

"During a certain period of my life I attracted some rather bizarre characters. The reason was quite obvious. I was behaving like a bizarre character myself."

—Liz Renay, *How to Attract Men*

sweet sweeney agonistes

This is not a book about successful relationships, so I'm not going to bore you with stories about boyfriends. You didn't dole out your well-earned clams to hear about how blissful it is to wake up next to somebody on a Saturday morning, eat a frittata, go to the planetarium high and make out during the laser show. What I *will* regale you with, in keeping with thematic schadenfraude, is a story about how shitty it is to break up with somebody you did, at one point, love, because you were given the chance—and then things changed.

PATRICK AND I dated for a year, and had delirious, retarded fun together, and then he moved in with me, and we had one more year together after that. Because we were both in our mid-twenties—I was twenty-six and he was twenty-three—nothing we did had any import beyond feeling good the moment we did it. But he was able to make me laugh so hard I cried, and we liked hanging out with each other all the time, and for a while it was all euphoric and silly, with the low stakes of youth fueling the time we merrily killed. We were high constantly, we performed for fun, and neither of our jobs mattered. It was like Narnia, or Neverland, or Ork (is that a fake place where things are great?). It only took two years for the reality to settle in that our relationship was not good for me: I wasn't doing what I needed to do when I was Patrick's girlfriend. I was too lazy or fucked up to write anything that was any good or to have any ambition beyond throwing together a sketch or short film here and there, and every day Patrick went to sit at a desk at a job he couldn't stand, then went and did improv onstage with his friends at night, and I'd resent him for not wanting more than that. And I guess I felt entitled to judge his fulfillment as well as my own because we were basically married, which is what it's sometimes called when people live together, don't date other people, and share living expenses.

Toward the end, our differences were racking up, and I knew I didn't want to end up as his wife—not "be" his wife, but "end up as," because, like I said, he was twenty-three, and twenty-three-year-olds usually don't get married unless they live within twenty miles from where they grew up. I knew Patrick and I were not going to make it to grown-up land after I went home with him for Christmas and landed up to my tits in culture shock, and not in a fun "I'm on safari!" way, but in an "I don't want this for the hypothetical children I haven't even decided I want" way. I witnessed his family's exchange of large-ticket electronics and stocking stuffers after their "drop in whenever" Christmas Eve party, which was unheard-of to me, having only celebrated appointment-only family gatherings centered around brisket meals for a definitive amount of guests who come at four and leave at seven.

I remember Christmas Day, the last one I'd spend with Patrick, and going to his uncle's basement to sit around two fold-out tables shaped into an L. The men talked about sports and pulled from their Silver Bullet tallboys as I pushed my ham around my paper plate and waited for somebody to talk to me or at least embarrass me, like I was used to. I remember thinking at the time how far that basement was from Scarsdale, which all of a sudden seemed, like they say in that song, "At The Ballet," if not like paradise, at least like home.

So gradually and inevitably, Patrick's and my bond dissolved. He drank, smoked, and ate more, and I started to nag him about the symptoms of his unhappiness. We stopped having sex, and I bought a king-size bed so we could sleep next to each other without touching. Patrick started snoring and picking fights with me about how he thought circumcision was institutionalized genital mutilation, and there seemed to be points of contention at every turn. Patrick was a tech genius, and the TiVo he'd made from scratch by soldering a chip onto his Xbox had a glitch and would record his shows only— episodes of *Law & Order & Penn & Teller: Bullshit!*—and never my episodes of *The Comeback* or documentaries about cults and sea mammals.

We respected each other's sense of humor, but we didn't regard each other so well in the "every single other department" of being a person. It pained me to make room for Patrick in my apartment so he could store his ugly sweaters in the dorm-furniture-style dresser that ended up in my tiny bedroom. I didn't want to throw away my cute TV to make room for his behemoth thirty-inch monitor—the one with that Franken-TiVo attached. I hated his food in my fridge. I hated his Warren Zevon poster on my wall. And even though we didn't speak much about our relationship, Patrick—an Irish Catholic guy who regarded the concept of getting into therapy as absurd of an idea as my ever getting out of it—told me something sad that resonated, toward the end.

"Every time you talk to me or say anything at all, it's like there's a silent 'comma, you asshole,' after it."

And he was right.

I didn't love him enough to be a good girlfriend any more than he had the ability to love me enough to grow into the kind of partner he knew I needed. What started as a chummy alliance with a best friend you have fun making out with devolved into constant rounds of bickering with an alien you resented because he kept you from the enjoyment of the world's getting the full benefit of your ambiguous "potential."

During the second summer I spent on vacation with his family, Patrick and I sat on the beach after a walk. I'd watched his brothers and sisters light fireworks the night before while I sat a safe, Semitic distance away from the explosions, my hands folded in my lap. As we sat on damp sand and the tide got low, I suggested to Patrick that we try to live separately and see what it was like to take that step back, but still be "together." We weren't breaking up; he would just move out, and maybe our relationship would go back to being fun, like it was before we got to know each other better.

That *always* works! Because time goes backward, not forward—right?

He thought about it and later agreed that the plan made sense, over pulled-pork sandwiches at a shoreside BBQ joint, the mascot of which was a cartoon pig wearing a chef's hat, jollily searing the flesh of one of its own.

A month later, Patrick and his stuff were gone from my apartment. And not long after that, I began exchanging daily e-mails with a Broadway actor I didn't know, on whom I developed an obsessive crush. I was handling the not-breakup very well, or the Irish Catholic way of "not at all." Who said the Irish were the only group immune to psychotherapy? Was it Freud, or Freud via Martin Scorsese in that ham-handed movie *The Departed*? I've always found the Irish really attractive—they make wonderful writers and sexy firefighters, and if they didn't like the Red Sox they'd be perfect. But their "not dealing with stuff" thing may have been contagious, because I handled the dissolution of my living situation with Patrick by not handling it, and instead decided to pour all my energies into corresponding with an Equity actor I had only met once; and at the *stage door*, for Christ's sake.

I SAW a production of *Sweeney Todd* right after Patrick moved out, and fell for the guy in the lead role, all right? And I wasn't critically appreciative from a safe blogging distance; I was bludgeoned and ravaged into crazytown by this seemingly random performer who shook me into fandom at an age closer to thirty than twenty. It was embarrassing: I hadn't written love letters to a celebrity since I put purple ballpoint to pink legal pad to tell the actor who played Wesley how cute I thought he was in the very special AIDS episode of *Mr. Belvedere*. And then there were those humiliating incidents of me being way too into sketch comedians in high school, confusing what I wanted to be one day with who it might be fun to have sex with. If Dana Carvey, whom I am certain is a fan of female-author-helmed dating memoirs, is reading this one, I just want to say, "I hope you weren't too freaked out by the birthday card I sent you when I was fourteen, or allergic to the Opium brand perfume it was marinated in," and also, while I'm at it, "I really liked your performance as Pistachio Disguisey in the motion picture *Master of Disguises*."

Only today, in the cool, Catskills-crisp air of retrospect, can I now see that my fantasy-fueled correspondence with a Tony Award–winning triple-threat Demon Barber of Fleet Street had its roots in a few different pots of batty soil.

People who love theater are often cynical, despite or maybe because they know they're capable of being so moved by the experience of watching a play that it feels better than real life. But it wasn't enough for me to enjoy that guy's performance the night I saw his show. For some reason, I had to read his bio, find his website, get his e-mail, send him a note that dropped the names of friends we had in common, and then, upon receiving a personal response, pore over every last word, intention, and emoticon until I had whipped my lady parts into a meringue-like frenzy pie. What was I, Kathy Bates in *Misery*? Or *About Schmidt*? Which was the one in which she was naked, and which was the one in which she bludgeoned James Caan? She lives out the fantasies of so many women, that Kathy Bates. God bless and keep her!

Our e-mails weren't just an isolated incident of fan mail, either. I had a good month or so of back-and-forthing with my Broadway beau. Note—this is a legal concern to add this, per the request of the actor I'm writing about. He'd keep writing back and I'd keep putting myself out there: sending photos, inviting him to rock shows, to coffee, stopping short of asking him to shave and eat me. *[Broadway Joke Alert!]* I acted like a retard tween, and this after two years of bitching about being with a guy not as mature as I was.

But Sweeney kept hitting Reply, and he was as flirty as a pleated skirt every time he wrote back. It's a no-brainer that actors have to flirt with everybody to maintain a level of success. When your product is your own face, voice, and body, you need to maintain a sense of charm and fuckability to make yourself special beyond the sum of your parts in order to remain employed, even at the expense of the otherwise attractive assets you might be lacking, like smarts or good jokes. But my critical filter was as broken as the one on the humidifier I don't clean as I pored over Sweeney's correspondences each morning, enlisting a team of my most sympathetic friends on e-mail forward patrol, designated to tell me things I wanted to hear, like "He wants to get together with you, it's just that his schedule is crazy," and "He signed it with an 'x'; that means he wants to kiss you." I'd think about him every night before sleeping, and wake up every morning before peeing to run over to the computer and check my inbox for the latest from Sweeney.

And all the while, I lived in the acupunctural tingle of anticipation, hoping that one day we would go on a date in real life, and that it would be as fantastic as it was when I saw that show. Meanwhile, I did not go out on any actual dates.

Then, one day, I woke up, and there was no e-mail from Sweeney. He stopped responding.

AS I mentioned before, I don't usually spiral into extended periods of delusional quasi-stalkery. So in an effort to map my madness, I should mention another variable, besides Patrick's moving out, that, at the time, didn't seem to have any connection to the blossoming romance in my mind.

The day after I saw *Sweeney Todd,* and a week after Patrick moved out, my father's mother, Adele, to whom I genetically credit my inability to reasonably function anywhere besides New York City, my exaggerated sense of stubborn self-sufficiency, and my love of '70s clothing—particularly the cowl neck–medallion pairing—passed away, at home, after suffering from a long illness.

The week after my grandmother's death, Patrick didn't call me, visit my home, or write me to express his condolences, because, as he would later explain, he knew my family was sitting shiva, and didn't know whether reaching out was in line with the Jewish rite of mourning. (It is, in fact, sort of the point.) Another culture gap was accumulated between me and ol' Patrick, and this time, it was a bigger deal than ham on a paper plate in a basement.

Eventually, I forgave him for sending a card to my parents after the fruit baskets had rotted and the veils on the mirrors were lifted. He would tell me later that he was sorry that he didn't know what to do and that he didn't err on the side of kindness and generosity. I acknowledged that the timing of our discovery that "moving out but staying together" was a veritable Fudgie the Whale of a lie that we pretended was a real possibility at the time of our transition-easing. But our rift stung as it revealed itself in the face of a loss of a family member I'd looked up to for as long as I was alive. And I don't look up to people just because I share a last name with them: Adele Klausner was the kind of person you identify with so totally that you see what you like about yourself in them, and it makes you think you're all right by association.

Adele was the one who would take me to the New York Public Library and make me walk five blocks to Ray Bari pizza afterward, which felt like the Trail of Tears to a suburban creampuff used to riding five minutes to get to Italian Village. She survived breast cancer before it was a cause you wore a ribbon for, worked for the Nurses' Labor Union until retirement demoted her to commie volunteer, and taught the aerobics class she took at the 92nd Street Y when the teacher was sick. She'd bake her own pies from scratch and wouldn't let me win at cards. She lived alone in a high-rise apartment building and walked three miles every day, even if it was shitting sleet. And when she said she loved me, she smiled with all her big teeth.

Then, one day, she was gone. And so was Patrick. I lived alone, and I was trying to get used to it. As I moved furniture around and threw things away, I thought about the advice my grandmother had given me a year earlier, when I told her I was moving in with my then-boyfriend. Patrick and I had been looking at apartments in the East Village together, and considered pooling our rents for a bigger place instead of making room in my one-bedroom for his stuff. And Adele said to me, with the authority of a woman who had lived alone in Manhattan since her husband left her a widow at forty-two, "Don't give up your apartment." It was the best kind of advice—prescient and blunt.

I missed her and Patrick like crazy, but I didn't like thinking about it. My mind was far more content to spin sultry yarns about an actor I hoped would ravish me with the same conviction he funneled into his bloody stage performances. It's unwise to underestimate the macabre fascinations of a grieving mind or the sexual fantasies of the recently heartbroken.

SINCE OUR one-way obsession-fueled exchange, I've met Sweeney a couple of times. He's always been extremely kind to me and has never mentioned the e-mails, which I appreciate. Read from top to bottom, I'm sure they make a clumsy bit of fan fiction, collaboratively penned by two people well-versed in theatrics. But at the time, they kept me, if not sane, at least more human. And I see Patrick all the time, since he quit that job he hated to do more of what he loves. We're not friends, but I still like him.

People forget in the moment that breaking up isn't an action; it's a process. Not a deus ex machina, but a whole show, and a big one too—the kind with time elapsed and flash-forwards, and sometimes a stage manager has to put talcum powder on your head to age your wig. It's not just a click of the mouse to change "In a Relationship" to "Single," or the command "Send," when you're trying to tell Sweeney Todd you think it would be fun to have coffee sometime. It takes a long time for relationships to shift their contents, and then change their very makeup. Before Patrick and I had that conversation on the beach, I'd been quietly packing up the stuff that belonged to him, in my head. And not just his dresser. I was picturing what it would be like to come home to just the cat, cook for myself, date other guys. By the time we talked about him moving out, I had some of my feelings in boxes already. It wasn't easy, but it got better. Not every breakup is scored by Tina Turner and ends with you wiping your hands, "That's that." Adult relationships, even with guys you think are immature, dignify more gradual separations. And mine from Patrick took a long time, even after Sweeney and Adele were gone.

YEARS LATER, Tim Burton's film version of *Sweeney Todd* came out, starring Johnny Depp. I liked it, though I'll never understand the goth inclination to erase all humor when adapting to film what is technically a musical comedy—as though jokes and tan skin together are responsible for everything that's offensive to people who like The Cure. But it was awesome to see that story told on the big screen, and it was a pleasure to hear those soaring, familiar melodies in surround sound while throats spurted and roaches scurried into pies. I also realized, watching Depp do his best "Bowie Todd," that I was super-attracted to him in a way I'd never been before. I guess I'm one of the rare girls who never had a thing for Johnny Depp—weird, I know: Even lesbians like that guy. But I had a crush on Dana Carvey, remember?

But Depp as Todd did it for me, and when I figured out why, I had the kind of moment that makes you actually surprise yourself with how nerdy you are. I realized when I saw that movie that I, in fact, have a crush on Sweeney Todd. The character. It sort of made that whole mystery of "Why me, why then, why him," when it came to that actor, a cold case. Because "him" could have been anybody in that role, to some extent. A ton of guys like Catwoman, whether she's Eartha Kitt or Julie Newmar, right? I guess I just like Sweeney. Is that the worst thing in the world?

As I watched Depp croon to his razors and waltz with his conspirator, I thought of the guy kind enough to e-mail a lonely girl who liked hearing him sing. And then, I thought of Patrick, and remembered, as I do every day, my grandmother—the one who made her own pies from scratch.

the critic

Alex and I met online Christmas Day, because the only thing more festive than rallying around a tree with loved ones is frying your eyes by the glare of a laptop screen alone in a dark room, because all your friends are out of town, and you're bored to tears in the house you grew up in, and the loneliness of not having somebody to love during the holidays rapes your face every quarter hour, on the hour.

This was my first Christmas alone for a couple of years. The year before I'd gone home with my then-boyfriend to listen to his mother read a "letter from Santa" to her full-grown kids, citing their accomplishments of the past year. She/Santa referenced me to Patrick when it was his turn, adding, "Well, well, well!"—Santa always exclaimed in threes—"It looks like you have a special visitor here today!"

A year later, I was home with my own family and

online in my brother's old bedroom turned mom's new office, looking for faces on what was at the time a gleaming new social networking site. There's always a pathetic glint of "Now It's Different"–based optimism when you get a new toy; as in "*Now* I'll be able to find the career I always wanted," or "*Now* I'll be able to lose weight or find a guy to fall in love with" as soon as you get access to a new job counselor, exercise gadget, or website you hope will bring you closer to the dreams you've had since you were old enough to want things. They keep you from thinking you're the same as you ever were and spare you from the responsibility of being at fault for not seizing the opportunity of your surroundings.

As it turns out, in fact, meeting Alex on MySpace was only one of the electronically conceived disappointments I've endured while embarking on the task of finding somebody to love me by typing into a box that plugs into a wall. If I ever meet you, I'll tell you in person about the time I went on Match .com and met a chess enthusiast whose ability to bore adults to tears just by saying his own name ("Herb") was eclipsed only by his racism toward Mexican busboys. The two of us will laugh, and then one of us will cry, and then I'll go home and eat frozen waffles.

Around the time I met Alex, MySpace was exotic and alluring: I spent a lot of time that Christmas weekend arranging my "Top 8" friends for my brand-new Comedy Profile, and I put my friend's band in the first row, because I thought that showed off how cool I was. But that only took thirty seconds, even with my parents' crappy internet connection, and in that time, no exciting stranger had found my profile and noticed how cool I was. So, I set out to click around the site's expanse and soon found myself sifting through the pages of my friend's band's "friends." Maybe there was somebody else who liked this band who would think I was cool. After all, we liked the same band, right?

Go ahead and reread that paragraph and hit yourself in your own face with a frying pan every time you read the word "band" or "cool." That's an approximation of how embarrassing it is now to look back and see the criteria that fueled my search for a life partner. Because, in truth, I only *sort of* liked that band. I wanted a new boyfriend, I wanted him in the time it took a page to load on Safari, and I was excited at the possibility of this sparkly new website being the missing link between me and the person I always wanted to find.

Alex was friends with my friend's band. I found a thumbnail photo of a handsome, sharp-featured guy wearing glasses when I perused that page, and I clicked on him. He was even better-looking when the photo got bigger. I saw more photos of Alex. He kept getting hotter. Everything about his profile looked great, but that's because I was skimming it for references. He seemed funny. He liked the same TV shows as me. But according to the location underneath his age, it said that he lived in Tulsa, Oklahoma. What? Why? That was weird. But maybe Tulsa wasn't *that* far away. Was it? I had no idea. I'd never been there, or looked for it on a map. I decided not to worry about it, and clicked "Add as Friend" under his handsome face, thinking it was like throwing a seed out the window of a speeding car, with limited investment in the possibility that it sprout into a tree one day. I got a message back from Alex within the day: "Hey, funny girl."

And then the seed became a tree.

WE E-MAILED back and forth for a while, and that lead to IMs, then texts and calls. He found my website and he liked my work, going as far as to pay me what was the ultimate compliment coming from him: "I keep getting indicators that you might be the female version of me." And on the surface, we did seem to have a lot in common, but only in the way I scanned his profile for proper nouns, like bands and movies. Alex was a music critic and a pop culture savant, which I loved about him, but I was also at a stage where I didn't realize the relative importance of things like musical taste and opinions about TV shows in the grand scheme of two-person compatibility.

After our first phone conversation, I wound up at a party at the apartment of one of Alex's New York friends—another fan of that same band, which seemed to attract a lot of people of a similar ilk. Bands are social; they're not like comedians. Band members hang out with one another after shows, and there are parties and hookups and fun and other things that make me nervous and sort of jealous of people less neurotic than me. I guess it's why I glommed on to those guys, groupie-style, after my breakup. It all symbolized some kind of social opportunity. And nobody will go to as many parties or be more open-minded to hanging out with random jerks as the recently single. People who've just gotten out of relationships are constantly trying to prove to themselves how much they were missing out on before.

I was psyched to be at that party, even though I was flanked by a bunch of hipsters with whom I'd never be able to sustain a conversation longer than "Cute shorts," "Thanks." But at least I wasn't home alone, online. I called Alex the next day to tell him how funny, what a coincidence, and pretended that I hadn't gotten a wretched impression of that whole scene. I felt like now I was *in*, even though those people—his friends, I assumed—were alien and awful.

Soon, Alex and I were talking on the phone every day. I got to know his routine; he would take me with him when he went to buy his menthol cigarettes at the Circle K, and I would talk to him on my walks home from shows. We would text each other constantly while we watched the same thing on TV. We got to know one another, sort of, and I became comfortable chatting on the phone beyond figuring out a time and place to meet up, which is what I usually use the phone for, when I'm not texting. With Alex, I'd created the perfect boyfriend whose only flaw I could think of was that he couldn't touch me, and I would voraciously debate people who wondered if I chose him because intimacy freaked me out.

You can't say something that direct and honest and totally true to people in a long-distance situation. They will get defensive, and tell you all they want *is* intimacy, only they've been painted into a corner of having to cope with the God-given circumstances of not being physically near the person they want more than anything. But those people are full of beans, and so was I. Distance was what I wanted and needed at the time: the perfect conversation *was* the perfect boyfriend, and that's what Alex gave me, often.

I loved talking to him. I snapped to attention when I saw his name lighting up my phone screen, and we spoke every day, and before we went to bed—sometimes until my phone got hot against my cheek.

Alex had an amazing speaking voice, and he'd call me

"babe," in this flippant way that was so sexy I wanted to kill myself. I didn't have experience taking to guys who didn't hem or whine. Maybe it was the Southerner thing. Alex was irresistibly gruff and deliberate, and even when he made jokes you could hear in his tone the makings of that wrinkle he had in all his photos: the little vertical line in between his eyebrows, a result of knitting them in terse thought.

I spent my days in reverie, thinking about how one day, Alex would be in New York, and how we'd fall in love, and we'd be able to call it that, because we'd be off the phone and in person, like real couples who live in the same town and know what it's like to look at each other's actual faces, and not at their photos, when they're talking. Oh, and there would be bonkers sex. Because this guy was—by *far*—the best-looking guy I'd ever had any kind of interaction with in my life. At least that's what it seemed like from his photos.

Obviously, there were huge gulfs of difference between us that extended beyond physical distance. But unlike Patrick, whose Santa-channeling mom gave me the "I Don't Belong Here!" jitters, Alex's Southernerness drove me bats in my pants. He told me that he was a bad kid in high school who got into trouble a lot, hoping that it wouldn't "freak me out," which it didn't, unless "freak me out" was slang for "ruin my panties" in his part of the country. He talked about himself—his goings-on, his worldview, his opinions—and I took it all in the way geeky kids read comic books. He had stories about going to this party, or seeing this band, or bartending this wedding for his catering job, and even the mundane stuff about his life seemed like field reporting from Where the Cool Kids Are.

For everything he had to say, I was at attention; rapt and flattered that somebody as hot as Alex was paying attention to me. I mean, he was just so fucking hot. I was used to "quirky-looking," or "funny, so it makes him cute to me." This guy was just out of my league.

I tried so hard to show Alex that I knew about stuff too—I could reference old movies and albums he thought were hilarious. I made jokes and laughed at his, even though they were more referencey than funny, as in, "Look at how I remember this terrible band from 1978!" or, "Check it out! I've seen *Cannonball Run*!" He wasn't funny the way people who can really make me laugh are funny—people with a surprising insight, a unique point of view, or access to footage of a cat falling into a toilet. I knew I was funnier and smarter than Alex, but he was cooler and way better-looking, so I tried as hard as I could to use the resources I had to make him like me.

After three months of whatever long-distance intimacy we'd established, I gently initiated more provocative conversation. I didn't start a phone-sex session or nothin', but I made sure he knew, in my inimitable way, that I was growing impatient for him to fuck my mouth before it got warm outside. I told him before going to bed one night that I had a double-D-cup bra, and I remember hearing his voice waver, and then get quiet in a way I hadn't heard before. I didn't want to keep pressuring him about when he was going to come and visit me, because he dropped the subject whenever I did, until I finally said that if it was about money, I could pay for his flight. I don't know why I said that, because I couldn't. I was in grad school for illustration (which is a genius idea if you want to make money and also it is Opposite Day) and juggling two part-time jobs. But I had some savings, and I was dying to meet him. I was also eager to classify his reluctance to set a date and time as something that had nothing to do with his being too nervous to go through with meeting me in real life. It was more attractive to me that he was broke than scared, though it turns out he was both.

Alex called me back the morning after I described my breasts and asked if I was serious about buying him a ticket, and that's when I realized he was shit-poor. But that revelation receded into the background so "The hot guy is coming to New York!" could take center stage. I went ahead and bought him a plane ticket.

All of my girlfriends told me not to do it, that it was doomed. But Nate understood—he'd seen Alex's photos too. And I knew deep down that it made sense to fly him out here because I wanted that badly to see what he was about. But Project Alex had only made me crazy, not stupid. I was still wary of a thirty-two-year-old man who couldn't afford a domestic plane ticket with five weeks' notice.

Those five weeks went by like the last two hours of a temp's workday. We texted each other more than we usually constantly texted each other, about how much we couldn't wait, how we wanted "this" to be "something," and other things you say to strangers you're convinced you will love soon but do not want to scare with soothsaying.

THE DAY finally came, and Alex texted me from LaGuardia Airport after he landed. We were to meet at a bar on Avenue A, with no presumptions that he'd spend the night at my place, as per my friend Angie's advice, and, to her credit, "You met him on the Internet! He could be psycho!" is never a bad thing to be reminded of. The plan was that Alex would drop off his stuff at his friend's apartment, then meet me at the bar and "see how things went." He told me what he'd be wearing so I'd recognize him, and I wore a top over a bra, instead of something strapless, because he'd told me how much he loved unhooking lingerie. I probably shaved my legs four times that day, and got my hair and makeup camera-ready. I walked over in my cute wool coat, even though it was puffy-jacket weather, and when I realized I was there early, I walked a lap around the avenue, warming up for the big event.

I cornered the block to find Alex through the window, inside the bar. I saw him tiny at first, then big when I walked in, like when I clicked from his thumbnail on Christmas to see the big picture. I met eyes with a stunning, oddly familiar face. And I was so relieved. Because, in the Mannerist tradition of the whole affair, I took one look at Alex, and I knew I'd done the right thing. I'd been vindicated. Even though he was short—and I mean, like, *Dudley Moore*–short—Alex was, true to the Internet's assurances, indeed, so. Good. Looking. I was literally agog: meeting eyes with Alex was like seeing a work of art look back at you. I marveled at his features like I was ogling some kind of tiny, expensive bird.

"Hi."

"Hi."

There was nervous laughter, and he looked down at his hands like he warned me he might do, in one of our phone calls from the week before about how we thought it was going to go. After some chat about the movie they showed on his flight, Alex broke down and told me I was "really pretty," and hearing that made me feel like I was drunk, it was such a sweet relief. That whole evening was fast, fizzy, and happy, and I jubilantly experienced whatever the opposite of "regret" is about spending money on his ticket. He wasn't a rapist, I decided, so we walked down Avenue A back to my place, and he kissed me really gently when we got upstairs. I was ecstatic, and then he spent the night.

"Spent the night," so you know, is not a euphemism in this case. There was no making out, and certainly no sex, but the evening's main event—finding out Alex was attractive in real life and that he thought I was too—was enough of a high for me to spill the news to my friends about how explosively my Tulsa boyfriend lived up to my shallow expectations; he wasn't ugly, and he didn't butcher me into a torso and leave my limbs in a trash compactor, so I figured it was time to show him off, like an imaginary friend whom suddenly everybody else could see. Handsome-face's deb ball awaited!

I found out about a going-away party that was happening the next night and decided to go, even though I couldn't have cared less about the girl who was moving away. I think I was relieved she was getting out of town, frankly. But I knew there would be people I knew at that bar, and I wanted them to see me with a gorgeous date. And sure enough, I got a lot of compliments that night about how cute Alex was, and then, later into the evening, I found myself asking my friends at the party whether they thought, based on his body language, he liked me. I guess he was a lot less forthcoming in person; the stuff he would text me about wanting to cook for me and how beautiful my eyes were seemed like something I'd dreamt now that he was here. He wasn't touching me or kissing me even casually, and I wasn't sure when or if that would change. He also had that cool-kid affect; the kind of "mean" you see in teenagers able to make emotive dorks and weirdos feel they don't belong with an eye roll or a raised brow. Alex wasn't mean—not to me—he was just a little icy and withholding. And I was starting to feel insecure—like I needed more next to me than just a pretty face that I ordered online.

Over the four days he spent in town, Alex guest-starred in my ordinary life. He wrote record reviews while I went to work or school, and he came to see a show I was doing at the time. He told me how excited he was to see me onstage, but he showed up late, and because I didn't know whether he was seated in time, it totally threw off my performance. But I forgave Alex the instant I got to see him afterward. Men know this, but the charge you get just from seeing a beautiful face looking back at yours can be enough to make you overlook fatal flaws.

We went out after the show to a bar with Alex's New York friends, and they were just like the ones at that party I'd gone to before. You know: the jerks? Everybody was beautiful and acid-reflux-inducingly cool: These were the teenage bullies who thrived, and could afford to extend their adolescence. They had trust funds and vintage boots they don't make in my size, and bangs down to their eyelids and part-time jobs at record shops. I felt like I was in high school again—and I *hated* high school. I don't trust anybody who didn't. But that night at the bar, I felt formidable by association, and happily shelved my contempt—I was wearing cute clothes, I was the thinnest I'd ever been in my life. I felt like an alpha bitch, but I knew it was all fake and temporary. Those weren't my real friends, you can only maintain a weight you're not meant to be for fifteen minutes tops, and Alex was going home soon. We cabbed back to my place and slept next to each other for another platonic night.

★　　★　　★

AT THIS point, it was officially getting weird. Alex wasn't touching me at all, and now that he was in New York, he could. I didn't want to mention anything, because if I've learned nothing else from Martin Lawrence's stand-up it's that (a) men hate talking about stuff you think is going wrong in a relationship that you're not sure is actually a relationship, and (b) women be shoppin'.

Either way, us not having sex didn't make sense. It had been a few days in person after a few months of talking on the phone, and Alex and I were sharing a bed and nothing else. I was taking extraordinary pains to make sure I looked presentable before going to sleep next to him: I remember applying concealer, blush, and eye shadow before bed. I actually pulled my version of the "stretch, then put your arm around a girl at the movies" trick, getting under the covers next to Alex in a bra and panties, complaining how hot I was, then peeling my underwear off. But my nudity inspired nothing from the cherubic castrato to my right. I curled up, felt bad, then drifted off with a sorry pout on my powdered face, like Buster Keaton in the throes of another pitiable folly.

We went out to dinner on his last night in town, and to break up an awkwardly long silence over the appetizer course, Alex made me guess why he liked Caesar Salads.

"I give up." I said. "Why?"

"Because I hate tomatoes."

IT WASN'T that we weren't getting along—it was that I was trying like a champion to avoid any kind of conversation about just what the hell was going on between us. I thought that me talking about the tension, rather than him causing it, was what would ruin everything.

The next morning, before he left for his flight back to Oklahoma, I finally asked him why we weren't having sex. I wasn't asking for my money back, though I guess we sort of did have an unofficial arrangement for fees paid and services unrendered when I bought his ticket and put him up. Not that he was Deuce Bigelow; I just wanted an explanation before he was gone again.

He got instantly defensive, like he'd heard that question before, and told me that when it came to "the sex thing," he needed to go slow with people he liked, because it was "all really intense." Then his brown eyes met mine, and that's literally all it took for me to back off. Yes, really—I was actually flattered! All I needed was the reassurance of his pretty face for me to back off. I filled in the blanks, assuming that he meant what he didn't say: that soon I would be his girlfriend and he'd move here. I'd conveniently omitted the possibility that the man of my dreams was a eunuch or a closet case.

We said our good-byes, and soon he was back home. He texted me from Tulsa that he missed me already, and that he'd be back to see me again soon.

ALEX AND I spoke for two more months before he figured out a way to save the money he made writing freelance reviews tearing bands to pieces and tending bar at sweet sixteens to buy himself a ticket back to New York. But during the time between visits one and two, I was talking to a different Alex. From his phone voice, it sounded like the line between his eyebrows had gotten deeper from stress. Now he was grappling with adult stuff, like money and work and where he wanted to be and what he wanted to do, I guessed, in order to be with me. He seemed to want to change his life, to move here and write for a living and, you know, "succeed," but he seemed stuck and scared. He wanted to be in New York, he said, and I was happy to hear him starting to think that way, but I knew to judge only action, and he wasn't taking any, besides buying himself another few days with me. I forwarded him apartment notices and job openings, because I was trying to help. And I was told to chill out by the same friends who called me a moron for buying him a plane ticket in the first place. But I kept doing whatever I could to get him here. Meanwhile, I was in a Long Distance Not-Relationship with a guy who wouldn't consummate what we *did* have when he was here. I had no idea where I stood with Alex, whom I basically fell for twice—once online, and then in person.

Around this time, I got a job as a writer's assistant on a TV show. I gave notice at my other jobs and took a leave of absence from grad school to finish my MFA on my own. When I told Alex the good news, he asked me, "Are you gonna forget about me now? Are you gonna move on to something bigger?" And comments like that, no matter what the tone of the person who's supposed to be kidding, are never a joke.

Alex's second trip heaved with more urgency and anxiety: It was not romantic. I set him up with friends of mine I thought could help him get work in New York, and got out of his way when he needed my apartment to himself to write. And this time, his bags were at my place, where he stayed. But again, there was no sex. None at all! I would get naked and paw him at night over his T-shirt, kissing his neck, and he'd tell me to stop. I was confused and angry. I thought he wanted to be here, with me.

★　　★　　★

"WHAT'S GOING on?" I asked him in the morning, which is when straight guys will have sex with you when you're in bed with them and you're naked. He did that thing he'd done all week: looking at me, but not in my eyes. He was struggling. He blurted out something fast, about how the whole situation was really freaking him out. That's all he could say. He seemed mad. "I'm just really freaked out," he said again.

It was freaking me out too. I was so nervous putting my hand on his shoulder while he sat Indian-style at my feet watching *The Gong Show Movie*, wondering if he'd squeeze me back and whether it was sexual if he did. If I should kiss him first and what I'd do if he said no or pushed me away. I was awash in fear and self-doubt. Where did I get the idea that I was good enough for somebody to move to New York to be my boyfriend, anyway? I was becoming more and more infatuated with Alex, with or without sex raising the stakes, and his ambiguity was bringing out all of my most distorted, outdated perceptions of myself.

"It would be one thing if this was your rebound thing, after Patrick moved out," my friend Brandy told me. "But he isn't even *fucking* you? He's useless to you. *Useless*. Send him back to Tulsa and you're *done*."

She was right—what could be more useless than a long-distance, platonic relationship? This went deeper than my own problems. Obviously there was something wrong with Alex beyond his not being super into me—even gay guys let you blow them in the morning.

ALEX WENT back home, and a couple of texts and calls followed after his second trip, but none of them were sweet like they were when we'd first met online and were both infatuated with the potential of the whole thing. He told me how stressed out he was, and that he didn't know what he was going to do about moving here since his trip had left him broke. He wasn't happy in Tulsa, but he didn't know what was next for him. And even though he didn't spurt overtures in my direction like he used to, he kept calling, assuming I was committed to talking to him no matter how the situation shaped up. But I had already made my decision.

He *was* useless. I could make myself feel bad—I didn't need an unrequited crush for that—and I could sleep with the cat if I wanted to share a bed with someone who wouldn't fuck me. I didn't want to be his friend, and I was tired of pretending I thought he was funny. I was sick of playing fan-girl to a cool kid with no libido, who lived in poverty across the country. It was hard to figure out, because I liked him so much, but I *was* better off alone. I called him after work one night once he was back in Tulsa, and told him exactly how I felt while he was here, so he would know.

I SAID I wasn't stupid: that I knew he wasn't really in it to move here, to be with me, to take that leap. I made sure he knew that when we were in bed together and he didn't look me in the eye, it crushed me. It made me feel invisible, like I was always afraid he'd make me feel—just like, or even because, he was afraid I'd one day move on to something bigger than him. He curled up to me as close as he possibly could have in my bed, and he still wouldn't touch me. And there I was, naked and thin and warm and twenty-seven and double-D'ed and freckled and *his*. I shoved to the side that there was no way we could have ever gotten together without having to worry one day about my supporting us both by pulling in some kind of crazy Manhattan double income, or giving up on the idea of ever having kids, or not depending on my parents to help us out. I didn't care that he wasn't as smart as he pretended to be, or confused hating everything with being funny. I just wanted to kiss him; I wanted to make love, in the truest sense, to a person I already felt so close to. And Alex couldn't even deal with a blowjob. That fucking coward.

I said what I had to say, and he said he had to go and think, and I said good night, and then, the next day, we had our final phone conversation, in a private conference room at my work, after Alex left a couple of self-pitying messages about how I probably had him on pay no mind list and had moved on—like *I* was the one rejecting *him*, paging Dr. I Don't Think So. I called Alex back and asked him if he'd thought at all about what I said, and he asked me if I was giving him an ultimatum: that if we weren't a thing, or if he couldn't move here, or definitively be with me, whether we were going to keep talking.

And I said no.

And he said "ever?" And he was mad, and I choked back tears, because I knew I had to end it, like when you have to put a suffering animal to sleep so you can put it out of its misery. And I swear to God, I'd never in my life ended anything I wanted the way I wanted Alex. I wanted him so badly. I didn't think I would ever again find anybody I'd be able to love the way I knew I could love him. But I knew the reality of the situation, and that what I wanted wasn't going to come true. That the pursuit of it was only going to cause more pain.

So I said, "No, never."

And then he hung up.

douche ziggy

Here is a short list of what crazy people are good for.

1. Writing great fiction in the Southern Gothic tradition
2. Knitting outfits for their pet chickens
3. Boosting sales of Purell (for destroying germs), tin foil (for hat-making), bathrobes, and lipstick (for bathrobe-wearing and lipstick-smearing, respectively)
4. Shooting presidents

Sadly, however, crazy people also have a fifth use. And that is:

5. Providing otherwise reasonably functional people with crazy sex, which is not *just* sex with a crazy person, though it certainly is that, but also sex that is, by its nature, insane.

Even nonsexual human interaction with crazy people can cause people to become temporarily crazy (think about your family); but crazy sex with crazy people can make regular people *totally fucking lose their minds.* And all you can do once the sex stops and you've come to your senses is look back and retrace your steps to figure out how it is you got yourself into that mess in the first place.

I HAD an eighth-grade history teacher who wouldn't make us memorize any dates. She figured it was useless for us to know that the Magna Carta was chartered in 1215 or that the Treaty of Versailles was signed in 1919. Instead, when it was quiz time, she'd give us a list of events and test us on our ability to rearrange them in the order they happened. The time line, she reasoned, would be of more use to us than anything else, because the only way to make sense of history is by studying its cause-and-effect cycle.

I got into a situation with a crazy person named Ben because I had the loss of a damaged person named Alex hanging over me like a dirt cloud over Pig Pen for what had ballooned into a six-month funk. Alex's frigidity, after the sex-free final year of my doomed relationship with Patrick, plus all the time invested and the chocolate-chip scones downed in their respective aftermath, honed me into the perfect vessel for Ben's brand of crazy. Alex was Mrs. O'Leary's cow, I was the lantern he kicked over, and Ben was the Chicago Fire.

★   ★   ★

TEN POUNDS heavier from sadness scones than I was when I was wasting my time talking to Alex, I was only being productive in the moping department of my life, and the only writing I did took the form of boring journal entries about what a terrible person I was for not eating more salads. The days were getting shorter and colder, and the writer's assistant job I'd been working on for the past eight months had ended, and I suddenly found myself fat and alone and not over Alex one bit. But I decided I would try to quit being so narrow minded, and try to be "open" to men in my life I already knew but had never previously considered as potential romantic partners. That's right! I would do that! It would be a method known more commonly as "rooting through the garbage," but at the time I was certain it would solve my problems.

I'd known Ben in passing for years and never regarded him in any way beyond thinking he was friendly. He was a little heavy, but kind of cute. He was someone I'd say hello to in passing—a friend of friends. That's it. I saw him one night after a party I forced myself to go to, and when I went outside the bar to hail a cab, he talked to me while he smoked a cigarette. We talked about *Nashville*, and Karen Black, because Karen Black should always be talked about, and then Ben told me that he remembered meeting me six years earlier, and recounted all the details of our first encounter. He knew where we were, who we were with, how I made a joke about the Holocaust being fake. It jolted me; I didn't remember any of that, but his story seemed to check out, especially because the Holocaust is *totally* fake, and most of the time people think I'm joking about it. I was really flattered Ben remembered all those details about meeting me, and that he was, I gleaned, "open" enough to tell me about how he did. I thought he was really sensitive.

A week later, I wrote Ben and asked him if he wanted to watch a Robert Altman movie that we discussed when we were outside.

HERE'S THE thing about Robert Altman. His name is a cultural talisman; it's a topical buzzword for attracting the attention of a male adult of a certain age and cultural disposition. Some women learn about sports so they can seem interested in the Giants at a dive bar in Midtown, and others take the cultural approach. Altman is like Stanley Kubrick or Tom Waits or other men who make art that men like. I like Robert Altman fine. *Nashville* and *Short Cuts* are great movies, if a little long, and nobody is going to argue with Elliot Gould in *The Long Goodbye*. But I didn't really care about the movie Ben was telling me about that night. I was open to watching it, but my e-mail to him was more about me saying I was open to getting to know him.

I know. If you hear the word "open" again, you're going to *open* your mouth so vomit can spill out of it into the terlet. Well, ditto, dollface. I'll hold your hair if you'll hold mine.

Ben replied to my e-mail, saying he was happy to hear from me, and invited me over to his apartment in Astoria, Queens. And then, I decided to like him. He was funny over e-mail, and he mentioned details that "cool people" usually skip over, like how he didn't really have any food in his house except for wasabi peas and Beaujolais Nouveau, which he knew was sort of gay, and then he gave me really extensive directions to his neighborhood and told me to call when I was downstairs. And I was really charmed by how he typed out his train of thought: It was an affectless way of flirting. Again, I thought, he seemed really sensitive.

★   ★   ★

I SHOWED up to Ben's place wearing jeans, a T-shirt, and a hoodie, which, for me, is an unheard-of outfit to wear unless I am taking a trip to the county dump or giving a cat a bath. But I didn't want to break out a dress and tights because I didn't want him to think I'd made up my mind that I was attracted to him, even though I already sort of had, and I also didn't want to look like I thought we were on a date. Because we *weren't* on a date. We were just hanging out.

When I came into Ben's apartment, I took in all the books on his shelves and the movies in his collection, scoping out the semiotics of the place, and decided it was all very acceptable and impressive. Again, it was the cultural-literacy thing. I didn't care about college degrees and good breeding in terms of parents and towns. I was looking for the pedigree of taste, and with Ben, I thought I'd found a quality contender.

Ben was loquacious and polite. He spoke constantly and enthusiastically about the movies he showed me and the art he'd hung on his walls, and we got to know what we each thought was *cool* over what soon became hours.

Finally, around four thirty a.m., he stood behind me as I sat watching a YouTube video on his computer, and put his hand on my shoulder. It was the first time he'd touched me all night—that's how cautiously he set the stage for maybe later making his move, with permission. I didn't flinch, so two hours later, he finally lowered his voice and said how he was thinking about wanting to maybe kiss me if that was OK, and I smiled and nodded, like "Fucking finally, jackass," and the next thing you know, he'd gotten me onto the floor, flipped me over to all fours, pushed my panties to the side, and started aggressively lapping at my ass with his tongue like he'd been thinking about doing it for the last six years.

This was surprising.

At first I was embarrassed, because I hadn't shaved or showered right before, and didn't expect to be in the throes of such graphic intimacy when I headed out to his apartment. I was wearing jeans, remember? But when you're digging into the carpet and somebody's been eating your ass for ten minutes, your inhibitions and expectations shift considerably. Soon, moving into his bedroom seemed like a reasonable thing to do, especially since it was getting light out already.

I got under a filthy black comforter in his tiny, dark bedroom, the corners of which were graced with stacks of dusty old issues of *Penthouse*, and told Ben with no uncertainty that I was not going to take off my panties. He said fine, and we made out more, and then he was behind me, feeling my tits under my bra and rubbing his dick against my ass, and then I felt him push my thong panties to the side and slide inside of me. He started fucking me, muttering the whole time.

"It's OK, Julie. I left your panties on. Your panties are still on. It's OK."

I was deliriously turned on. I'd gone from no sex to crazy sex, and it was not healthy. It was setting me up for a crash, like eating a huge pile of candy after fasting for a week.

I WOKE up a few hours later to find Ben on his couch in a flannel bathrobe. I guess I'd banished him there during the night because his snoring set off my sleep-talking tendencies. He was smoking and drinking freshly microwaved tea—there was no food in the apartment, and the idea of him running out to get us some bagels seemed like something I'd be crazy to ask for. He seemed pretty settled in, like he wouldn't be leaving the house anytime soon. He puttered around, stalled and tethered in his own space, like a dog in its crate. There were no snacks in Ben's cupboards and the fridge was empty. For a fat guy, it seemed a little weird—I wondered when it was he actually ate food.

There was more sex after no-breakfast, and then I began getting ready to head out in my jeans from the night before. We shared our niceties about how it was a lovely evening, and what a great surprise and all that. He gave me a hug and I combed my hair.

And that's when he told me he was seeing someone.

"SO," HE said, like an afterthought, while I was getting my stuff together to leave, "I've been dating somebody for a while. But it's pretty casual. She doesn't mind if I see other women."

He cleared his throat and took a sip of tea, then continued, as calm as a pond, like he was about to ask me if I knew the weather. "How about you? Are you seeing anybody?"

My stomach lurched. I needed to go out and get food.

"No," I said. "No, I'm not seeing anybody."

And I was shocked. Not because I figured Ben had been waiting around his whole life for me, or at least since we met and I made that (hilarious) Holocaust joke, but that in the wake of what was an oddly direct disclosure that he was dating somebody, more than anything, I just couldn't believe that this guy wasn't completely available. As in, totally alone. It was kind of his *shtick*. When we were hanging out on the couch the night before, his gratitude for my company was almost overbearing. Who'd have gotten any whiff of unavailability from this guy? It was so masked by desperation musk the night before.

"I CAN'T believe you know about *this* movie!" he'd exclaimed hours earlier, exalting something off the radar in, like, 1991. He'd made me feel so high-status—I was the awesome babysitter with boobs and Van Halen tickets, and he was my adoring charge. And now, after a night of ass-pounding floor sex, he popped a "B.T. Dubbs" and told me, "P.S. I have an open relationship with a person you haven't heard of until now."

I had to go. Nate was dating this guy in a gay choir (don't ask), and I had plans to accompany him to Grace Church to watch his guy sing Christmas Carols next to a gaggle of other mustachioed songbirds, because I am the World's Greatest Hag. But Ben kept telling me more about the girl he was dating as I put my coat on, and that's when I found out that not only was Ben crazy enough to be telling me all this stuff with no shame at all, but that the girl he'd been seeing was a bisexual vegan who volunteered for PETA, and she'd been dating him for a *year*. I couldn't even react anymore at this point. I was just stunned, and didn't know what I needed most at that moment—an omelet, a nap, or a gun.

But Ben was surprised that *I* was surprised to learn all of this. He said he thought I knew about her. I asked him how, and he said it was because when I was working at my TV job before, I was in charge of maintaining the guest list for our wrap party. And because he was invited, and he told me at the time he needed a "plus one," I should've known from his RSVP that his "plus one" was his date. Meaning, that he and his "plus one" were dating. He told me that he'd introduced me to her, which I did not remember. That he said, "Julie, this is Leah, Leah this is Julie." And that I therefore had no reason to feel shocked and upset and hungry and bewildered and oddly betrayed by the events that had transpired over the course of the last twelve hours of my life in an apartment that looked increasingly disgusting in the light of day.

But I tried to ride out my first wave of "should-feel." You know when you first hear bad news and your first reaction, for some reason is, "OK," right before you flip your shit? Like you're told you're fired, or your parents are dead, or the test results are positive. And you know that in a moment or two, it's going to be a shit show, because honest reactions come from the gut once the brain has chewed and swallowed. But during the seconds it takes for you to hear the words—you practically see them, like they're in a cartoon coming out of a silhouette's mouth and landing in your ear—you think to yourself for a split second: "Maybe I can deal with this." And "Wow, that's a surprise, but maybe it will be all right." And then, finally, the unhealthy one: "Ooh! *Drama!*"

ONCE I left Ben's apartment, I tried to digest the news he'd broken while I watched Nate's Tenor with Benefits warble *"come let us adore him."* I tried not to think too fondly on the sexual acrobatics of the night before, as you do when you're convinced you're tits-deep with a Trouble Guy and you don't want to let yourself enjoy liking him so much before it's too late.

I didn't hear from him until six days later. While saying I don't want to be too judgemental at this point in the book is akin to somebody who wrote an auto mechanics manual saying halfway through they don't want to prattle on too much about cars, I still have to say that it made me feel bad to go almost a week without hearing from Ben. I know I was the one who let him fuck me, panties on or not, on our first "date" after inviting myself over, but I still think that once you sleep with somebody after a night of *heavy talking,* or pretty much in any scenario where you have a feeling the other person might like you above and beyond what could have just been a blowjob in a bar bathroom after doing lines, you should really be in touch with them the next day, if only to dispel the likely impression that you made on the person you spent the night with. If you don't get in touch at all, it's a shitty way of communicating your disinterest in any sort of relationship, by way of not communicating. And if you wait to call six days after the fact to bemoan at length how you should have called sooner, like Ben did, you're just not being a mensch. By then, I was in the position to decide if I wanted Ben's mensch-less, non-exclusive company, and its ensuing crazy sex, over no company at all.

And, guess what? It turned out that I did.

BEN SAID he was going away on business that week, but that he'd like to get together that Saturday. And I didn't hear from him again until Friday, when he called me over and over again from the airport in Dallas, where he was working, desperate to see me that night. I had dinner plans, but he kept saying how badly he wanted to see me, like he wasn't going to relent. He called again when his flight was delayed. And when it finally arrived at JFK. And then he whined to me about how badly he wanted me to come out to his apartment after my dinner. He would not let go of his argument. I told him no, let's do it tomorrow when we could have a proper date, like we'd originally planned. And he said no, he had to see me that night. I told him if he wanted to come into Manhattan, he could. And he said no, he was tired from traveling and I had to come to him because it was urgent and he wanted me. And against the advice of a restaurant table full of friends, and how he made

me feel the morning after our first night together, and everything I know that makes sense, I went out to Queens to see
him again.

I am not defending my decision. I look back and am floored
by the stupidity of it all, and the only way I can explain it is this:
Think of crazy sex as some kind of bug that somebody plants
in your brain. The bug then eats you from the inside out until
you're stupid and making the decisions of a raving lunatic made
almost entirely out of genitalia.

I TOOK a cab out to Astoria, where Ben attacked me in his
stairwell. We had sex again, and it was so great that I remember
thinking it was probably a dream that he told me he was seeing somebody else when we got together two weeks earlier.
Another woman didn't seem possible in the wake of all that
simpatico intensity.

I teased him the next morning, asking him when he was
going to take me on a proper date. He said he would come
into Manhattan later that night to take me out, and I think
that made it easier for me to leave. That, and I was starving and
there was still no food in his apartment, and seeing Ben in his
flannel bathrobe was giving me an unsavory bit of déjà vu. Was
this how he functioned all the time? How did he manage to
get himself to the airport and catch a flight to Dallas? And he
seemed to adore me, at least from his phone call from before,
with all its heaving desperation. Why didn't he call me the day
after we slept together? What the hell else was he doing at the
time? The only good thing about dating a self-declared loser is
that you figure the guy at least isn't too busy for you.

Later that evening, it wasn't until I was dressed and ready to
head out when Ben called to cancel what would have techni-

cally been our first date. He said he underestimated the amount of work he had to do, and that he couldn't come out to Manhattan. And now I was pissed, because I went out of my way to cab over to his place for sex the night before, and he couldn't even come out to Manhattan and eat a burger with me in public? I spoke to my shrink about it, and she told me, based on knowing me for the cartoonishly extensive, Alvy Singer–like duration of our therapy, that I should cut Ben loose. That she knew me too well to advise me in good faith to date a guy who was already seeing somebody else.

I happen to be a very jealous person, and I am not interested in learning to chill out in any way about that particular part of my personality. It bothers me so much when I hear about a man cheating on his wife, or stories about girls who give guys they're dating his super-unique fantasy of having sex with two women at once, or when girls fight over or compete for one guy, that I am actually getting angry just typing this right now. This might be sci-fi of my own design, but I think men should compete for the attentions of women, and that's sort of that. I may speak from a place of curmudgeonliness, but the opposite feels unnatural and gross to me, like the mint gum they make that also tastes like fruit. The idea that Ben had me and this other girl on his social burners at the same time drove me insane. It was a deal-breaker, ladies! I couldn't casually start dating him knowing that, and what we were in the thick of already was no longer casual. Hot sex is not casual. It begets legitimate feelings of warmth and attachment, even when the person giving you the sex can't give you anything else.

So I planned to stop seeing Ben. But before I did, I told him to come over to my apartment that Sunday night. Do you know why? Because my vagina is an idiot. But in addition to that, here is what, instead of logic, was running through my brain.

1. I wanted to break up with him to his face.
2. I wanted to make him get off his ass and travel into Manhattan, just like I cabbed into Queens a couple of nights earlier, like a *hooker*, against the advice of my friends.

And this is the most embarrassing reason.

3. I wanted him to come into my apartment and decide he liked me—the way I decided I liked him when I walked into his.

It was the cultural talisman thing again. Part of me thought he would fall for me as soon as he saw my books and my DVDs and all the cool shit on my walls, and how neat and clean everything was and how good it all smelled and how comfortable my bed looked and how awesome the music I picked out was. And I guess I hoped that he would see all that and decide to not be a huge mess of a man.

So, I was not thinking clearly. I wasn't able to see that the crazy Ben made me wasn't even close to the kind of crazy he had in him. And it was around this time when I realized that "crazy," in Ben's case, was not the thing Patsy Cline sings about, or an adjective that describes the hotness of chili. But Ben was a sick guy so devoid of empathy that he was unable to understand why telling me about a girl he was dating after sleeping with me would hurt my feelings. All of the clues were there. Colombo—the *yogurt*—would be able to solve the riddle. It would have just been sad if he wasn't so talented at making me so angry.

And that's just it—Ben had the skills of a savvy baby who knows just how to throw a toy down from his high chair until all you want to do is punch him in the mouth. But the baby will keep throwing toys because he knows you won't punch him, because only a monster would punch a baby. My interactions with Ben gradually turned me into a baby-punching monster. And I know where my culpability lies, so let's start with this: First of all, I shouldn't have ever had him come over to my apartment, if only because you don't break up in person with somebody you like sleeping with. It's dangerous. And if you do, you do it in public so there's no "one last time" sex, because that's like saying you're going to start a diet after you eat an entire pizza.

Because neither of us knew that, and neither of us operated on any kind of reasonable frequency at the time, Ben came over to my apartment that night in a stink about being "forced" to come into Manhattan. Like a filibuster champion, Ben argued with me for what became five hours about whether we were going to stop seeing each other. He blamed me for him getting in trouble at his work because he was late the morning after our last night together, and faulted me for making a big deal out of a thing that he said he needed to be casual. I told him how I felt, and it fell on deaf ears. It became more and more apparent that the other girl he was seeing was just the tip of an insurmountable, damaged iceberg. All bets for any kind of a relationship with him were clearly off: Ben was a dead end. But he was in my apartment and it was late. And then, I ate the whole pizza.

★   ★   ★

I'M SORRY to say it didn't end after we had sex that night. Ben and I kept sleeping together, and occasionally even going out on actual dates, for three more weeks. We spent marathon weekends watching DVDs and fucking each other, and when it wasn't horrible, it was fantastic. Because I'd caught his crazy, I relished how unhealthy it all was, and loved the crack high of getting laid. And the sex really was awesome. I mean, you haven't lived until you've let a bona fide nutjob drill your insides with his cock. Like, a real sicko.

Ben loved nothing more than putting himself down in somebody's presence. That was a perfect "conversation" for him. And in no way would he ever self-identify as a narcissist. Because in his mind, a narcissist is in love with himself. And even though Ben was obsessed with himself, he played the loser card like it was circumstantial. Poor Ziggy gets a sweatshirt labeled "One Size Fits All," but it's too big on Ziggy! I guess the world just fucking hates Ziggy. Ben was Ziggy, except a douche. He was Douche Ziggy. And Douche Ziggy mopes about, all the while bringing the worst possible fates onto himself while spending his time outlining their very design. You know that book *The Secret*? Ben was a walking (or napping) example of the anti-*Secret*. He'd call himself a fuck-up, and then he'd fuck everything up.

But he was also provocative: he loved a fight. I don't. It's why I can't watch *Fox News*, and I keep the comments turned off on my blog. It's a monologue, not a dialogue, goons! I also hate confrontations, and getting heated up until you're yelling at somebody who just will not hear you. And that's what our relationship was when we weren't fucking each other until our genitals resembled hamburger meat or agreeing that the movie we were watching was cool. And in the time we spent together, talking dirty on the phone, spanning hours without food, gazing into each other's eyes, grunting and pulling each other's hair, I managed to forget about that other girl. I figured she went away, just like I never really believed she existed in the first place.

In a way, even though we'd only gone out for a little over a month, I felt like I knew him and that we were close. We spent intimate time together, falling asleep in each other's arms, sharing personal details about our lives and our families. I couldn't imagine how he could be seeing another person on top of that. When would he have time? It didn't make sense.

ONE WEEKEND, after Ben spent the night at my place, we lay in bed together. It was late morning and I asked him what his plans were for later that night. He whined a noncommittal response under his breath, and I asked him again what he was doing. He said he was busy. And I pressed on, because now I was on a scent.

"What are you doing, later, baby?" I asked.

"I have plans," he said, which seemed insane.

He was always home when I called him there, and we'd spent the last three weekends together. I asked what kind of plans. And he whined like a child being forced to tell his mom why he didn't want to practice piano when he told me the following, in my own bed, while we were both naked.

"I can't spend tonight with you, sweetie, because I have a *date*."

And that. Was. It. I was suddenly sober. Something in my ailing brain snapped back into place with the accompanying *blam* of a cap gun being fired, and all of a sudden, I felt my crazy collapse into itself, like a demolished house, until all that was left inside of me was a single, raw nerve. And it wanted to kill the fat, nude jerk in my bed. It wanted to fucking *kill* him.

I got steely silent—the kind of internal quiet that makes men nervous when they see women go there, because it means they're stewing and plotting. And as I processed the audacity of the morning's events, I thought about that old fortune cookie game—the one you play with your friends at the end of a Chinese meal, when you add the phrase "in bed" to whatever's in your cookie? This guy—this fucking narcissist with the hygiene of the Unabomber—told me that he had a date with the bisexual vegan he'd been dating this whole time—*In. My. Bed.*

I GOT up and started putting my clothes on, and Ben frantically followed me into the next room. It was like he had to take a cue from my behavior to see that he'd done something wrong: He didn't know before I'd reacted that he said something he wasn't supposed to say. He begged me not to be mad, and I icily deferred, and then he got hysterical, hoping I'd respond, but I didn't. He wasn't going to defuse my anger, and he wasn't going to confuse me any more into thinking that I was as crazy as him. And then he made himself cry.

Have you ever seen a grown man in the act of working himself up into a lather so that he can cry real tears in front of you? It's an excellent cure for being attracted to someone.

Ben stood in my living room, squeezing out tears like he was wringing a damp rag, whimpering out everything he could bring himself to say except that he was sorry. He said he was "flipping out," that he "couldn't handle" it, that "What did I want him to do—lie?" It was all self-saving. It was what he had to tell himself out loud so he didn't have to face the possibility that he'd actually done something wrong. I watched him self-destruct with indifference. I wanted him to get out of my apartment. It was like I'd woken up from a nightmare, but I still felt complicit. Like I'd watched a scary movie before going to bed.

Later that day, I got rid of Ben for real, but he kept calling to argue with me about why I had no right to be mad, until I had to hang up on him. I made the mistake of trying to convince him that he was wrong and I was right, and you just can't do that. People like Ben just can't understand anyone else's point of view.

There's a test that was developed by a child psychiatrist named Piaget, where you show a toddler a three-dimensional model structure, like a castle, and you sit with him across the table and ask him to draw it twice: one from his point of view, and one from the point of view of the person across the table, who sees the castle from the back. But the kid will draw the same thing twice. He will draw, two times, what the castle looks like from where he sits. Because he hasn't reached the point in his development where he can imagine another person's perspective.

Ben didn't even try to see the castle from my position on the table. What he *did* do—aggressively—was try to be friends with me after the wreckage. He would send me long e-mails and leave me rambling voice mails saying he wanted to make sure I knew how awesome he thought I was. As though me being kick-ass was ever at stake in our not seeing eye-to-eye. And he begged me not to hate him. It made it harder for him to sleep at night knowing that there was somebody out there who knew his "sensitivity" only referenced his ability to bruise easily with standard handling. Because Ben's was not a two-way thin skin. He didn't have any problem hurting the girl smart enough to know that "Please don't hate me" is not the same thing as "I'm sorry." He just couldn't stomach the consequences: He could not be hated.

And I don't hate him. But I don't like him. And I don't have to. Of the many lessons one can learn from dating crazy, I've learned that asking Ben to be decent and empathetic was like asking somebody with two broken legs to run a marathon. He just can't, and it was cruel of me to expect that he could. But I also know now that there are some people who, even though they are low-status and should, by definition, evoke compassion, will instead bring out a side of you that is so sadistic, so eager to be mean and combative and other things that are not you, that you must avoid them altogether. These are the provokers—the ones who can't evoke pity because they're inherently infuriating. It's the woman at the gym who screams at you when you change the channel, or the old man who wanders around the park and gets mad because you're sitting on his bench, or that asshole baby who throws his toys.

There are plenty of troubled, cluttered souls who make you want to hurt them as much as they hurt you, even though you know they're already suffering plenty. The part of me that is kind sympathizes, because I know that as difficult as it is to be around someone like Ben, it's way more difficult for him to be himself. The part of me that still hurts knows the same thing, and takes comfort in the karma of it all.

giants and monsters

I was going to meet Greg at the bar again. He was home, visiting New York, and I hadn't seen him for years, since we used to sleep together, in my early twenties. Greg holds the distinction of being, to this day, the ugliest person I've ever had sex with.

THERE ARE a couple of advantages of sleeping with an ugly guy. First is the obvious: that if he's self-aware of his visual deficiencies, he might be nicer to you than a good-looking person, and possibly even try harder to please you sexually. This theory is in line with the water-tight one passed around frat houses that fat girls will "do more" in bed because they hate their own bodies and don't want you to leave them.

But the other attractive thing about ugly guys lives in the uniquely female part of the brain that makes sex with them exciting. Because just as men can be really turned on by the act of degrading a beautiful woman in bed—coming on her pretty face and generally violating her perfect body—some girls get off on the idea of letting a hideous monster have his way with them. It's a turn-on for some of us to be defiled in some way. If you try hard enough, you actually feel like a prostitute!

I hooked up with Greg on and off for a long stretch of time—we did not date. Greg was ugly *and* angry—a winning combination, only the opposite—and in no way did he want me for anything beyond the occasional last-minute night together, when he'd take me home with him and plunge his dry, plump fingers inside of me. After we'd sleep together, neither one of us would talk about it to each other or mention it to anyone else.

I WANT to clarify what I mean by "ugly," because it's a harsh word. Greg was heavy and tall, and he had sausage lips, tiny eyes, and a broad nose with nostrils you could see just by looking straight on at his face. He wore the kind of glasses you're supposed to get rid of in 1989 or when you turn sixteen, whichever comes first, and his hair was thick and curly, like a bush he'd pruned into the shape of a mushroom. Greg was pigeon-toed and his shoulders rounded forward, and he wore striped wool sweaters and pleated chinos with trainers.

Here is what he had going for him, and here is why I would sleep with him, which are two very different sets of criteria. Greg was big, so he made me feel small when he held me, and he did hold me sometimes after we had sex, and that was nice. He also had a soft, gentle speaking voice, and he was very funny. But, like plenty of funny people, Greg was unusually angry. He was constantly sarcastic and seemed to hate everybody, including himself, but he'd never talk about the philosophy behind his contempt for everything. He'd just alchemize his vitriol into a steady stream of droll put-downs, sometimes directed at me, and I don't know if he realized how mean he could be, or whether he cared. And I'm afraid the second grouping of Greg's qualities—the one that doesn't read as a list of assets—has more to do with why I let him take off my clothes and impale my pale early-twenties-ness on his big, chubby erection on a semi-regular basis over the course of a year, when we were both drunk enough.

Oh, we drank a lot then too. Greg would drink more pints at the bar than I'd ever seen anybody drink in one sitting, and then he would get flirty and handsy with me, and I remember thinking I was lucky when we'd end up sharing a cab back to his place late at night. He'd ignore my jokes or dryly poke fun of things I'd say in earnest, in attempts to connect, and I'd laugh when he made fun of me. We'd sit on his couch and watch *Conan*, and then we would start making out, and soon we'd go into his bedroom and have rough sex, and I have to confess, it was thrilling.

He would spank me and bite me with his liver lips, and bounce me up and down, and I'd watch his massive chest jiggle from the force of my body on top of his. I would bring myself to orgasm, because he never bothered, and I would think to myself, "How *perverse*! How *exciting*! How *kinky* and *exotic* to let a man grotesque enough to resemble one of Quentin Blake's illustrations of the child-eating giants from *The BFG* have his way with me, then snore himself to sleep."

THERE'S SOMETHING inherently repugnant about a naked man. Before you fuck a guy for the first time, the element of mystery is sometimes more scary than alluring before his clothes come off and he's up against you. His odors, his flab, his body hair—all those variables are all up for grabs before a man shows you what he has. I never clutch and tear at snaps and zippers: I do not undress men. I let them take their own clothes off, and hope there's dignity in their behavior when it comes to that part of the process. That there's no posing or flexing, no long drum roll implicit in the pacing of how he peels down his drawers. I pray that he isn't looking at my face, hoping to see in it the reaction of a six-year-old girl at her first Ice Capades. Meanwhile, men relish every detail of the reveal of a beautiful woman's naked body. They savor the observations of the kind of panties she has on, the unhooking, the unbuttoning, the gradual unveiling of the statue beneath the pretty silks draped on top of the alabaster undulations. But I just want to know what I have to deal with as straightforwardly as possible. What parts I'm going to have to pretend aren't there and which ones I know I need to focus on after making out stops being polite and starts getting real.

Men's bodies need to grow on you. As comfortable as men are with their penises, and as exhilarated as they are when they're tumescent and buried in a pretty girl's face, it is never not weird to be on the receiving end of the act, at least at first. I'm certain that even seasoned escorts have to work past their initial wave of reflexive disgust at the strange task ahead of them—sucking off a stranger—before they can dive in, and eventually even enjoy it. But it beats temping, right girls? Of course it does not. Get your life together, you whores!

Then, it's not the penis but what's around it that's always oddly off-putting in some way. Before you actually know and love him, I mean. Look, I'm hardly the first girl to say that balls are weird. Because they *are*. I don't know a single woman who can put at the top of her flights of fancy the task of sucking on her boyfriend's scrotum. I don't mind a pair if they're shaved or trimmed and tight—the kind that come with a lovely, massive erection—but I've always regarded balls the way I think about a boyfriend's brothers. You have to be friendly around them, but then you're secretly glad when they say good night after Thanksgiving and you don't have to hang out with them again until the next special occasion.

Even men I have gone on to fall in love with, and to relish every inch of their bodies—balls and A.H. included, because I am talking about *love*—have seemed foreign and bizarre when appearing naked in front of me the first time. I think boys grow up using pornography as a road map for what they should expect once they get a girl naked. They know since their adolescence precisely what they want to do to us, they like the idea of "ruining" a virgin, and they know when girls get naked that it will be mostly skin and no hair, because women are supposed to be perfect and smooth and soft and smell good, and we've all had practice sucking on tits since we were babies.

The male body is chaotic and obscene. It's funny like a monkey is funny, but if the man who lives in it is a good one, you can learn to love his body completely, like a tree you used to climb on as a little girl. But at first, seeing a man naked is like being cornered by some odd dog. And seeing Greg naked was always that: It never got better. I would habitually divert my eyes from his formidable love handles, which spilled out the waist of his Dockers like hairy pizza dough. I focused my attention on kissing his neck and ears and pretended the moles on his back—the ones sprouting long, coarse black hairs, like ponytails—weren't there. I'd close my eyes and take his fat, darty tongue in my mouth, and tolerate any incidental pain that came along with his gruff technique.

During my time with Greg, I would get off on being treated badly by somebody unattractive and mean. I would misinterpret what was going on between us as *sizzlingly erotic*. I cherished what I reckoned was an addiction to the S&M stylings of a true sexual artisan, who really hurt me when he spanked me, and took the whole "treating me like shit" thing beyond the bedroom, like when I'd see him at the bar some-times, flirting with other girls.

I didn't want Greg to be my boyfriend. I just wanted him to be nice to me in public if we were going to keep having sex in private, or maybe call me on occasion to see what was up, after he was done with me for the night. Then, one day, when he decided he didn't want to see me anymore—that it was over—I cried in front of him and asked him to reconsider. But he said no—that we were through. He was done and there was nothing I could do to convince him otherwise. I met him at a sports bar near my apartment and asked him to come home with me, but he said no again, and he was cold when he cut me off, like my pleas really disgusted him, and I didn't see him after that until years later, once he'd moved away.

WHICH BRINGS us to the embarrassingly recent past. It was between Christmas and New Year's when I met Greg, again, at that same sports bar, where I'd been drinking with friends after a show. I was thinner and had more lines around my eyes, but he looked the same, except he had grown a goatee, which is the worst possible thing you can add to an ugly face. Seriously: a hockey mask or a Hitler mustache are better alternatives. A goatee, especially on a corpulent man, is like a hair ring float-

ing atop a raw loaf of bread. Goatee-growers don't understand
that their beards do not obscure their double-chins—in fact,
they draw attention to them the way a red circle on a math
test shows you where you went wrong. Greg's goatee had some
gray in it, which reminded me of our age disparity. He was at
least ten years older than me, and when we were hooking up
like college students years ago, my only excuse of consenting to
being roughhoused so shoddily was my relative age and inex-
perience with good sex. But what was Greg's excuse? His being
old never meant, as I'd then hoped, that he was an adult. There's
a big difference between a "grown-up" and an "old guy."

Greg and I got to talking at the bar, and it got late, and he
asked if he could "crash on my couch," because he no longer
had a place in New York. And because it was raining really hard,
and for a lot of other reasons that have to do with going back
in time and taking the temperature of the person you used to
be, I said that he could.

He was polite in the cab, and there was no touching, but
as soon as we got upstairs, he shoved his tongue in my mouth
artlessly and groped me with the awkward passion of an entire
high school marching band. Which I guess I was open to, having agreed to let him into my apartment and knowing what
that meant, but I was surprised at just how awful his Shrek-like
hands and mouth felt all over me. It used to be different; I used
to like this.

I wanted to push him away, but then, suddenly, I felt the
status shift. Now I was the one who had more power than him,
if only because I'd belatedly realized how gross this all was. I
was older and, if not wiser, at least slightly less of a dum-dum.
Re-hooking-up with Greg, years after I'd had real relationships
with men who treated me well and good sex with guys who

did and didn't, made me realize how different I was from me, then. Because what was, at the time, I thought, a rough, kinky, exciting, crazy S&M relationship with a masterful pervert, was, in fact, just bad sex with a creep who had no idea what he was doing.

His paws groped me blindly and randomly, and I pushed him back and asked him to slow down. I tried taking the lead in the kissing, and closed my eyes so as to better pretend his floating hair ring was a full beard belonging to a forceful lumberjack of some kind, but to no avail. It was terrible. But when he asked to move into the bedroom, I said "OK," because "next" is always easier for me to say than "cut," and also, I was, at this point, getting a pretty remarkable education in how much I'd changed, and the only way to graduate was to totally concede to the revolting action about to unfold.

We got into my bed. Greg took his clothes off and his body was predictably abhorrent. And when I reached my hand down his boxers to see if he was hard, I felt a distinctly aberrant, raised area on the skin of his inner thigh, the hair of which had been totally shaved. I pulled my hand back in disgust, like I had been burned by fire, and decided the best course of action was to ignore it and proceed with the matter at hand, avoiding that area of Greg's body. After the most disappointing bout of sexual intercourse I'd consented to since college, I got ready to go to sleep, wrapping a towel around my neck, in line with my osteopath's then-orders. (I have a neck thing, it's boring. Basically, sometimes it hurts and I have to keep it supported at night. Now you know!) And Greg—the walrus with the gray-speckled soul patch and the demon growth on his shaved inner thigh—actually made fun of me when I put my towel on. He said I looked *stupid*. He was teasing me, but it wasn't playful—it was a distinctively ill-intentioned display of a person sneering at somebody who is nicer and better-looking than they are. Like Sarah Palin cracking to crowds in her RNC speech about Obama being a "community organizer." I tried hard to drift off to sleep before Greg so I didn't have to hear his snores, and in the morning, he showed me in the light what I felt underneath his boxers the night before. And it was terrible.

There was an extended, raised patch of black and blue where his leg met his crotch. It was dark purple and fuchsia and all these other awful colors, and indeed the pubic hair that crept down to that area was shaved bare. I felt my stomach lurch into the kind of panicked nausea you get when you accidentally flip past the medical channel on cable and you see somebody's eye getting sliced open, and somehow, there is *pus*. Greg's body was gross enough, but this new development was unfathomable. What was going on? Was he sick? Did he give it to me?

He told me that he came back to New York because he had to get a heart operation at Mount Sinai, and, for the procedure, the surgeon went in through his leg. His gory bruise was evidence left in the wake of the invasive tubes or needles a surgeon shoved up the rotting building that was Greg's body, in order to fix his weak heart. I wasn't surprised that Greg had cardiac health problems, not just because he was a heavy guy in his forties who drank a lot, but also because people that angry often get sick. It is a fact.

I quickly looked away from his scar, and from the incision on his calf, which was also shaved.

"It's pretty gross, isn't it?" Greg said, then pressed my fingers hard against his incision. I felt some other kind of firm protrusion underneath all that black and blue grossness and screamed, "Ew!" He laughed at me like he had the night before, and like he did all the time when we were sleeping together, whenever I'd try to ask him something personal or when I tried out a joke that he thought was stupid.

Greg didn't know how many times he'd brought me to the brink of shouting "Ew" years earlier, just by being naked. He didn't know that his ugliness only made a hook-up situation that was merely disadvantageous into something my young imagination decided was "perverse." That because when we were in the thick of it, Greg never let on for a minute that I was beautiful and he wasn't. Not even in our intimate moments did I ever wrench a single compliment out of him. And he never knew that because he never told me I was fantastic, I worked harder to prove to him that I was. Because twenty-two-year-olds, even the ambitious ones, don't have much else besides that to do. They like drama, and they need projects.

I got out of bed that morning, after jerking my hand away from the latest installation of the visiting horror show, and got dressed quickly, so he would know it was time to leave. He was starting to touch me again, and I had to get out of that situation as soon as possible, so I could start pretending it never happened. I showered with hot water as soon as he left, then took to the task of cleaning up my apartment.

I decided over the roar of the vacuum cleaner to never again allow him into my space. I'd worked so hard to rid my apartment and my life of people who habitually made me feel bad. Maybe I'd told myself that bringing Greg home again was a history lesson, but that morning, it just felt like a relapse. He was as gross as he ever was, only now he was actually sick. And how much had *I* really changed if I took him home with me and let him give me the business, as usual, but didn't even have the compassion to sympathize with what he'd been through after he showed me his wounds? I felt guilty for not giving him the same kindness I wished he'd shown me years ago, and foolish for putting myself into a situation I knew I'd outgrown. I felt like an asshole and a sap at the same time.

As I Swiffered obsessively, I wondered whether people like Greg could ever learn to be better men from others patient enough to teach him—and I thought about how relieved I was not to want that gig anymore. Because even if it *was* possible, I finally had better things to do with my time than roll up my sleeves and make a mess of myself trying to change what was wrong with him. After all, I thought, as I threw the sheets we'd slept on the night before into the laundry hamper, it took the technology at the disposal of a team of Mount Sinai's finest surgeons just to fix his heart.

SECTION FOUR
exile in guyville

"Sexual choice . . . is one of the only areas where women are indisputably in control. It's not until they've made a choice, and submitted to it, that the relationship is inverted—and the man is generally back in a position of power over her."

—Neil Strauss, *The Game*

"I want a boyfriend. I want a boyfriend."

—Liz Phair, "Fuck and Run"

paper clips versus larry flynt

I was at the after party for a low-rent awards ceremony at a comedy club, because my writing partner and I were nominated for a short film we made. She and I made a mockery out of the occasion, drinking from the bottle of Bacardi Light we brought along with us and heckling the presenters, and I ended up having a better time than I expected to, because I quickly got drunk. I know stories about "how wasted you were" are little-league, but the truth remains that when you drink, stupid things become silly, and who doesn't like laughing at things that are silly? That's right: nobody, and assholes.

I spotted a friend of mine, Wendy, at the bar when I went up for another round, and greeted her sloppily. We were chatting about her new boyfriend, whom she seemed nuts about, and because I have no boundaries, I pressured her for details.

She said they were set up by a mutual friend, and I interrupted, "Hey!" which is always a good conversational transition.

"You should set ME up with somebody," I realized in Wendy's general direction, loudly. Unfazed, she told me that she knew somebody fantastic.

"He owns his own company. He's got an amazing apartment. He's cute."

"Yeah, yeah, yeah," I responded. "But is he a pervert?"

At the time, I couldn't congratulate myself heartily enough for inquiring about whether Wendy's friend had the most important quality I could think of in a potential mate. I just wanted to make sure she wasn't grooming me for an awkward evening of polite conversation about siblings and *New Yorker* articles with a bore over drinks. I'd had my fill of arranged social time and didn't want to kill time in the company of someone who didn't know how to pull a girl's hair in bed. One guy I'd been out with recently actually tugged at the *ends* of my hair, not the roots, like a third-grader trying to get the attention of his babysitter, which is not how you do that.

I told Wendy, with Bacardi breath and no shortage of confidence, that I didn't want to waste time with the formalities of matchmaking unless I was certain there was a hungry, hungry weirdo with a prevailing fondness for deviant sex at the end of the equation. I sloppily detailed my demands, and my friend assured me that he and I were perfect for each other and that she'd give him my number the next day. I gave Wendy a hug, told her she was my best friend, and somehow piled myself into a cab.

Soon after, I got a call from her friend Josh. From our first conversation, I learned he "had a thing for redheads," knew Wendy from college, and laughed like "heh-heh-heh," which is how people let you know they're flirting, instead of expressing the kind of laughter you release like a sneeze, when you actually think something is funny. When I spoke to Josh, I didn't laugh either way.

He told me about his company, which he said did branding and licensing for "all different kinds" of products, but that he got the business off the ground when his company signed on a pretty famous porn star, whom he took credit for "making a household name." He put her likeness on clothing and energy drinks and hooked her up with spokesperson opportunities for mainstream brands, and now she was getting legit roles that didn't require double penetration and HD makeup for her asshole. Josh told me, maybe to seem like less of a sleaze, that he used to have a lot *more* to do with what he called "the industry," meaning porno. But he assured me that today he attended the AVN Awards each year just to promote his client's new line of erotic novels.

I guess that was why Wendy was so confident we'd be perfect for each other. I drunkenly told her I was looking for a pervert, and Josh was obviously comfortable with sex. In fact, it seemed like he still worked in the sex industry, but from the standpoint of making it *legit*. Much of his career, he said, was founded on the mainstreaming of sexuality, which is a nice way of saying he made porn more popular. And, on top of that, he was a nice Jewish boy who grew up minutes from my native Scarsdale. Even if this guy was the total square I suspected—AVN Awards notwithstanding—I was at least probably going to get laid for the first time in what seemed like forever.

When it came down to our making plans to meet, Josh asked me "what I liked to do," which seemed weird. Don't you just ask somebody for coffee or lunch before getting written confirmation that your date doesn't hate drinking or eating? I told him to meet me for a drink, and got to the restaurant he suggested to find a good-looking guy a bit taller than me in a newsboy cap drinking at the bar. He was wearing a vest, too, and a thumb ring, which is never OK, but I tried hard not to overjudge his overaccessorizing, and let him be nice to me, which he was. He was very, very *nice*.

For a guy who did so much work in the euphemistically generous "adult entertainment industry," Josh was shockingly dull. He didn't have much to say about our mutual friend except that she was "great," and he hadn't heard of the TV shows I wanted to talk about. He told me that he was close with his dad and wanted kids one day. He said he did yoga and tried to eat healthily. And when I asked him about his work, he bragged about being responsible for getting a travel kit with a vibrator, lube, and condom tucked inside a discreet makeup case sold at high-end Manhattan department stores.

He was, true to his goals of "mainstreaming sexuality," very comfortable talking about porn and sex, which are not the same thing. And even though he mentioned having been more professionally involved with porn than he was currently, it was clear that Josh still considered himself in "the industry." He wanted to talk shop about which actresses did anal and which only did lesbian scenes. He debated the merits of broadband versus DVD formats. And just like a teenager who'd fallen love with pot, it wasn't enough for Josh to watch the occasional dirty movie—he had to wear his vocation on his sleeve, like the seventeen-year-old who brandishes the culture of his chosen vice, buying marijuana-themed clothing and taking up hacky-sack. Josh had taken what was unspoken into what was everyday for a living, and "everyday" is, coincidentally, another word for "boring," which he was. We parted that night with a hug.

Josh called me a few days later, which was also very, very *nice*. It was clear he liked me and I appreciated that he followed up the way I think somebody should after a date, so I agreed to go out with him again. That's a rule I made up that I think is a good one: If I'm iffy about being attracted to somebody right away, but he goes about pursuing me in a way I think is upstanding, I always give the guy a second chance. It's a way to be strict about your standards, but open-minded about your contenders. Men are way more likely to become more appealing to you over time than they are to magically grow manners.

BEFORE OUR second date, Josh flirted with me in an e-mail, warning me that "If I was a good girl, Santa would bring me some presents." Both of us were Jewish, but maybe he thought it was sexy to refer to himself as Father Christmas, in the third person. This time we both had dinner, because I guess he assumed that dinner was something I "liked to do." He was right!

As soon as we sat down at our table, Josh gave me a shopping bag full of porno-themed comic books, tchotchkes with his porn-star client's face all over them, a copy of her erotic novel, and that travel kit with the lube and vibe inside of it.

"I figured it was too soon to bring you the big glass dildo from my office," he disclosed, tipping me off to his decision process and referencing our nascent courtship. "So I brought the travel kit. It's really high-end, and it comes in a nondescript makeup case, so it's *discreet*."

I intoned the same "heh-heh-heh" he gave me on the

phone, then watched Josh get way too drunk way too fast, which was embarrassing for both of us. He ordered sake, and fed me the cucumber garnish that came with it. The first time I bit into the cucumber, to be sporting, but the second and third time, I declined to play along, unwilling to stop midsentence to chomp on crudités.

Josh had a lower booze tolerance than me, which I did not believe was possible. It takes a Butter Rum lifesaver and a teaspoon of Dimetapp for me to wear a lampshade like a hat and forget I can't dance to hip-hop. But after two and a half sakes, whatever inhibitions Josh actually had melted away like a suppository, and as soon as we got outside the restaurant, he impulsively decided he wanted to take me to a movie. He leaned on my shoulder while I helped him stumble to Union Square, only to find the theater was closed, to Josh's cries of "Damnit!" He suggested we go to his apartment to watch a movie instead. Saying "sure" and meaning "why not," I hailed a cab and pushed Josh into the backseat. He was a mess.

I WENT back to his apartment and recoiled at its details. It was spacious and in a lovely building, like Wendy had told me, but everything Josh had added to it spoke to his poor taste. There was bad art on his walls, *The Family Guy* on DVD, and only two books: a vegetarian cookbook and the new Oliver Sacks in hardcover.

"How is *Musicophilia*?" I asked my gradually sobering date.

"Oh, I haven't read it," he admitted. "It was a gift."

Josh opened a red Netflix envelope and put in a DVD as I made myself as comfortable as I could on his deep velour couch. The movie he'd rented was a documentary called *Paper*

Clips, and it was about the efforts of an elementary school class in Tennessee to collect six million paper clips in an effort to represent, with office supplies, the number of Jews killed during World War II. Yes, that's the movie Josh chose to show me back at his place to set the mood for seduction. I'm as shocked as you are: Who knew they taught about the Holocaust in Tennessee?

He hit PLAY, and then began to give me a back massage, which is a coward's way of making one's way to the sexy bits that live on the front of a lady's torso. As his hands migrated over my shoulders and onto my breasts, the audio from the movie morally distracted me from being sexually aroused. "Josef Mengele . . . paper clips . . . millions gassed . . . about an hour from Chattanooga." The smell of sake on Josh's breath and the coldness from the metal ring he wore on his thumb invited the comparison to the film's subject as parallel atrocities.

I'm going to go ahead and say it: *Paper Clips* was a misguided choice for mood-making. But it was only Josh's latest in an evening-long series of gaffes. The booze at dinner enabled him to tell me, over my protests, about a three-way he had with two women that he swore was "the most beautiful, nonjudgmental, *natural* experience ever," which was sad and gross and not something I wanted to hear from a guy on a date, even if I *were* attracted to him. Josh just didn't know when to shut it. Now that we were back at his place, I just wanted to close my eyes and pretend he was somebody smarter, while I made the best of a mediocre date and let him feel my boobs.

I grabbed the remote and muted the movie when they started showing photos of the ditches the Nazis used as mass graves, because I am a *class act*, and then we started kissing. It was tepid and twee; there was a lot of caressing and ear-breathing. I kept my eyes closed after noticing the persistence of his moronic grin. Things proceeded predictably, until Josh took his pants off and I noticed that he'd shaved all his pubic hair. I credited his grooming choice to the double-pronged influence of watching a ton of porno and thinking too much about one's genitals.

Josh nodded at me while I beheld his shorn business with an imbecilic smile on his face, and maintained his facial expression as I removed my clothes, like I was stripping for a toddler with gas. I don't like smiling or laughing in bed, by the way. I'm funny in real life: When I'm getting fucked, I'm off the clock. I prefer a little reverent solemnity, like in church. But once I was naked, Josh piped in again with his "What do you like?" shtick, and I said, bluntly, "Coming."

I let him use the sex toys he got for me until I was done, and then began deferring his offers to sleep over. I didn't like him enough for that kind of intimacy, and if I wanted to wake up to a shitty painting of a flower pot hung on an exposed brick wall, I would sleep in a college town coffee shop.

As soon it was clear to him I wasn't going to be convinced to spend the night, Josh threw clothes on and insisted on walking me downstairs. I begged him not to, hoping he would get it that I was done. But soon, he had his Mets cap on and paraded me past his doorman, with whom he exchanged overly demonstrative pleasantries for my benefit. They high-fived each other, so Josh could show off how friendly he was with the guy who worked in his building. I wanted so badly to get out of there.

"Maybe I'll call you about Saturday night," he said, on what was now Friday morning.

"OK!" I said in an overly high-pitched voice intended to indicate an enthusiastically noncommittal "Maybe!" to an optimist, and "No, thank you," to the layman well-versed in social cues. Josh, who was not moderately versed in anything, took my response as a cue to *imitate* me.

"OK!" he said, the same way I did, only exaggerated, and with a "funny" face.

What was once neutral about him, then annoying, instantly became obnoxious. You just don't imitate people like you're making fun of them if you don't want them to hate you. He asked if he could put me in a cab.

"No," I said. "I live four blocks away." He insisted I call him once I got back to my apartment. It was, again, very, very nice of him, but at this point, his second chance was up.

I walked home feeling guilty and awful. Was there something wrong with me that Josh's offer to hail me a cab made me so angry? What was my problem, anyway? A guy asks me to call him so he knows I got home in one piece, and I want to puke on his shoes and flee the scene of the crime, maybe stopping at the good deli on the way home for a cookie. Is that normal? How was I ever going to find a boyfriend, a husband, or a man who might actually be a good father from the pool of guys I actually found attractive? Would the guy who told me to come out to L.A. so he could slap me in the face while I sucked his dick laugh patiently at my cousin Sherman's corny jokes on Passover? Would the guy who said with utmost romantic sincerity that "fucking me was like porno" be there to wipe down my sweaty forehead after hours of labor? To nurse me through panic attacks and career shifts and the alternating Saturday afternoons of crying in long stretches for no apparent reason other than that it's simply a part of a messy, human adult life? Here was a good guy—a *mensch*—with the libido of a teenager and a nice apartment who makes a good living, who wants to take me out on a Saturday night, and I couldn't even do him the favor of falling in love with him and teabagging his shaved junk.

I DID a lot of things in the mid-90s that were incredibly embarrassing. In college, I wrapped myself up in packing tape and read the last chapter of *Ulysses* backwards in order to get a passing grade in a performance art workshop. I took part in a potluck/play reading of an experimental musical written by a skater named "Piglet," which was based equally in part on the music of Frank Zappa and the aphorisms printed inside fortune cookies. I wore blue fishnet stockings with green Doc Martens. I ate a pot brownie and saw a film about roller coasters narrated by Harry Shearer at the Sony IMAX Theater, which I remember being deeply confusing. But I also made the foolish choice to connect deeply with a Milos Forman movie about a filthy pornographer. No, I'm not talking about *Amadeus*.

In *The People Versus Larry Flynt*, the handsome, charming Woody Harrelson plays the decrepit, revolting pervert who founded *Hustler* magazine, and Courtney Love, when she was an emerging actress instead of just a mess with a melting face, played Flynt's wife, Althea.

I remember nursing an adolescent infatuation with pornography when I first saw that movie in college. I was reading books mired in the philosophy of post-feminism, which bred in me a hefty contempt for the 1970s kind of feminism that held stripping, hooking, and posing for nudie photos as vocations degrading to women. "Don't you know how *empowering* being a sex object is," I would exclaim to sociology professors, expecting their hair to stand on end and monocles to magically sprout from nothing, only to pop out of their eye sockets in amazement.

Now my attitude toward pornography is markedly different; I don't think the insane amount of crazy porn that's instantaneously mass-accessed on a daily basis by men of all ages is so great for women, in general. Maybe I've gotten cranky in my old age, maybe I'm scared of the Internet, or maybe I've just concluded that life is harder for girls; that it's more difficult for us to rise to any sort of professional prominence than it is for men, or to be taken seriously if we're too sexy.

I'm not saying I don't watch porn. Of course I watch porn, because I am not a *nun*. And I don't watch "erotica" with a "story" or "period costumes" in it, because I am also not a *lesbian*. The stuff I watch is not stuff I would ever do in my life, but I also know the difference between what I want to fantasize about and what I want to do with my weekend. If I were going to watch a man and woman of average height and weight grope and fuck one another, it would be a waste; like shopping at a chain store when you're on vacation.

But I'm not *proud* of the porn I watch—I don't talk about it with people I don't know well or enjoy it in mixed company. I watch it alone or with a partner as a means to an end. I'd like to call my way of watching porn private or not a significant part of what I do for a living or who I am, but I *am* writing about it in a book, so I guess that's pretty public, even if I'm grappling with how I feel about it out loud, because it's complicated, Denise Richards.

But Josh's "making porn legit" day job, combined with his story about the "awesome three-way" he had, bugged me beyond the fact that his story was not a polite thing to be discussing on a date. Nice guy or not, Josh, I thought, was barely good enough of a guy to get laid by *one* woman.

EVERY ONCE in a while, you do something that you know you've outgrown, just because it gives you déjà vu, or you think deep down you haven't changed, or you're just desperate to try something you think would have worked at one time. When I was set up with Josh, I was playing matchmaker to the twenty-year-old college student who thought porn could start a revolution, but only if women "took it back," like we took back the night. Remember when we did that? And how afterward, nobody was raped?

In the final scene of *The People Versus Larry Flynt*, Flynt, paralyzed from having been shot in the face during his free-speech trial, sits in his living room, palsied and, ironically, unable to maintain an erection—the very currency of his industry! He wistfully views tapes of his late wife, Althea, who has long since died of AIDS. And as she wriggles around in her bra and panties in the grainy footage, Flynt hears his own voice in the background instructing his beloved, "Strip for me, baby. Strip for me."

When I first saw that movie, I was *devastated* by this scene. It documented, to me, what was then my romantic ideal.

"She was the love of his life," I thought to myself in between heaving sobs. "And now she's gone! But when she was around, and he could still get hard, they had filthy sex. And then, they fell in love, or what counts as love between a dallying pornographer and a stripper addicted to heroin."

In retrospect, the last scene of that movie was a cringe-inducing interaction between two unlikable characters, one of whom was portrayed by a woman who has made countless life mistakes, including but not limited to living at one time with Neil Strauss. But at the time, for me, Woody Harrelson watching Courtney Love strip may as well have been a Byron sonnet.

I've always wanted a loving relationship with hot sex. I didn't know at the time that when you hop into bed right away, it can make things more difficult. Not because spreading your legs sends out a message that you can be treated poorly, but because your expectations get inflated when you do it and it's good. Whether hot sex right away can flower into everlasting true love still remains for me to be seen, at least from firsthand experience. But what I do know is that that the opposite is true: a mensch is a schmuck if he can't fuck you well.

My sexual fumbling with Josh was lousy because I wasn't impressed by the guy attached to his dick. I can get a massage if I want my body to feel good; I don't want to fuck a guy unless I think there's a chance he may have read something other than a vegetarian cookbook in the last year. Or if his jokes are funny and his laugh is rare, or he calls me "kiddo" and it turns me into wobbly parfait. Or if his hand on my back feels like the relief of walking into a spot of sunny pavement; when all of a sudden, it's not as cold outside anymore.

I SENT Josh's call to voice mail the day after our night of *Paper Clips* and pubeless fumbling.

"Hey, Jules!" he said on his message. "I'm calling about our plans tonight."

What plans? The tentative ones I demurred, before I was imitated?

"I just wanted to see what you liked to do. Heh heh heh."

There was a pause. I sort of felt bad for him. But pity isn't sexy; it evokes a totally different kind of squirming. Josh's message continued. "You know, you don't pick up your phone a lot. I'm beginning to think you don't have a phone! Maybe you just have, like, a fancy answering machine!"

With my deletion of that message exited Josh—messily, loudly, but with good intentions. And the only time I think of him is when I open the drawer next to my bed and I see the travel kit he gave me—the one with the vibrator tucked inside of it. The design of the kit is indeed, however uncharacteristically, very discreet.

i don't care about your band

A cute musician named Jonathan sent me an e-mail out of the blue. We shared a friend in common, and he saw me sing the Waitresses' "Christmas Wrapping" one night in Brooklyn, at karaoke. He wanted to say hi, he wrote, but he was unshaven at the time, and didn't want to make a bad impression.

OK. Cute. Fine. "An admirer!" I thought. So far, so good. He was certainly good-looking, which Google found out for me: lanky, thin, straw-colored hair, and cheekbones that could lop slices off a block of Jarlsberg. Google also told me he was sort of famous. Google, you auspicious matchmaker!

Jonathan continued, in all lower-case, to introduce himself. He found my website, he said, and loved my videos. Great! So? . . . I scrolled over his rambling exposition, waiting for the payoff. Was he going to ask me out? He didn't.

"i'm at home absolutely spazzing out because we're leaving in a few days to make a record and i have to/really should finish a long list of songs. so, waving hello and/or re-hello! all the bestest, jonathan."

Huh? My enthusiasm tapered off. A hot guy in an indie band, well-known or otherwise, waved me hello and/or re-hello mid-spazz? And he was leaving in a few days to make a rock album? How old is this guy anyway? Nineteen going on forty? Still, those eyes drove me bananas and coconuts. He was really, really cute.

Maybe he needed a running start. I gave him training wheels and a ramp when I wrote back, making asking me out really easy for him. I even used all lowercase, mirroring his casualness.

"hi jonathan! let me know if you ever wanna get a drink sometime. it would be fun to meet up."

A relationship book I once read told women to use the word "fun" whenever possible. They claimed it had a subliminal, aphrodisiac effect on men, who want a relaxed, easygoing, friendly girl attached only to good times; the human equivalent of Diet Coke. This is the opposite of me: I experience separation anxiety at the end of every episode of *Top Chef.*

I half forgot about Jonathan after that exchange, but over the course of the next month, I got a few texts from him, reporting on his band's stay in the Pacific Northwest. I'd hear about how their album was going, the weather, and what he described as the M.C. Escher–like house they were staying in, which is the kind of reference a college student would make. I wondered if his love letters read like other descriptions of art posters you buy at Bed, Bath & Beyond. "I want to kiss you in a crowd in Times Square while I'm dressed up like a sailor!"

I never knew how to reply to Jonathan's texts. They were

postcards—he was broadcasting, not communicating. But I liked hearing from him, in the way somebody who isn't juggling a ton of other prospects will shrug, "better than nothing," and I wondered if he'd meet up with me when he came back to New York, or if he'd flake out. It was fifty/fifty with this guy: He was roundabout when it came to getting together, but pretty consistent about staying in touch, on his terms. I knew the odds of anything serious happening were slim, but I still wanted to go on a date with a good-looking guy who went through the trouble of getting in touch with me after seeing me sing in a bar.

While Jonathan was away, I did more research and asked my musician friends what they knew about him. Collette, a singer, told me his deal. "He's an indie rock dreamboat," she wrote in an e-mail. "His voice is transcendent and he writes lovely lyrics. He has a nice face, he has a kid, and he tours a lot. He's a star in his world."

I was surprised to hear he was a father. I was twenty-eight at the time, and I'd never dated a guy with a kid before—I didn't know whether I was OK with it at all, actually. "What's the kid's name?" I asked Collette. "Li'l Dealbreaker?" Plus, from what I gleaned so far about Jonathan, he seemed like sort of a kid himself. Babies having babies? Somebody tell Tyra!

SO HERE'S the thing with me and musicians. I know most girls go crazy for frontmen who close their eyes when they sing and nod their heads when the drums kick in, but I'm like Shania Twain with that stuff. *That don't impress me much.* I'll take somebody funny and brainy over a peacock with perfect pitch any day. You can teach a monkey to play the guitar, you know—and, as a bonus, watching him do it is *hilarious*.

Still, anyone who can make a living doing something creative is impressive. And that, reader, is the single most Jewish
thing I've said in this book so far.

"*Nu?* He can make a living doing what he loves! That's a
successful man! What—would coffee hurt?"

Finally, I can't emphasize this enough: Jonathan was *extremely* attractive. He did, like Collette said, have a nice face. I'd
take her word for it about his lyrics, though, because I tried to
listen to a couple of his songs online, and I got too bored by the
melodies to pay attention to his words. It was typical indie rock
stuff: droney, thick, exhausting; but obviously heartfelt. Bring a
book. I tried to get to the end of one of his tracks, but a You-
Tube clip of a Basset Hound taking a shower was too tempting
not to switch to, mid-verse.

A couple of months after he contacted me in the first place,
Jonathan texted me when he was back in town, and asked me
out for that Monday. I said yes, and he wrote back, asking, "actually, are you around tonight?"

"No," I said, with a capital "N" and punctuation, belying
my prior casualness. I felt like a mom establishing boundaries
around a ten-year-old who already makes his own bedtime; too
little too late. I heard back an hour later: "monday it is!"

He already annoyed me, and we hadn't even met each
other. I would soon learn a lesson men have known for years:
it's possible to be attracted to somebody you don't like.

MAYBE "DON'T like" is the wrong term; after all, I was still
meeting him for a date. There was something I found clum-
sily endearing about him; or maybe it was just his looks. He
was really handsome, like I keep repeating. And I don't think
looks are perceived to be as big of a deal for women, who are

supposed to be immune to something as shallow as beauty. But the eye wants beauty, and what's the eye a window to, again? Apparently, the groin.

Jonathan's hair, the clothes he was photographed in, his smile, his symmetrical face: they were all signifiers. False beacons asked me to give him a chance. Don't you want babies with that nose? Don't you want to fall in love with a guy who looks that good when he smiles? It's science: We want to mate with hotties. Finding out that somebody good-looking is bad news is always somehow surprising, no matter how many times you learn it. It's like when you were little and you found out that candy was bad for you. "How is that possible?" you thought. "It's so *sweet!*"

FOR OUR date, Jonathan told me to meet him off the Bedford stop of the L train in Williamsburg, Brooklyn, where he lived, and thought I did as well. When he first e-mailed me, in fact, he suggested, "if you're in later and want a low-key indoor or outdoor hello from a neighbour (maybe?), that would be ace."

Jonathan's British spelling of the word "neighbour," his use of the adjective "ace," and his proposal that he come over to my place for the occasion of our first meeting were all putz alarms. But what annoyed me most was his presumption that everybody he thought was cool lived in Williamsburg. I had to live in his "neighbourhood," because, to him, I was obviously another girl planet in orbit around his star. In fact, I am a proud Manhattanite. And while Brooklyn is great for certain things, like dog-watching and artisanal chocolate, is there a Russ & Daughters in Brooklyn? A cab right in front of your building when you're running late? A single Broadway musical? No. And, more to the point, I do not live there. But Jonathan sure did! And, to the credit of his cheekbones, I still wanted to meet him.

After we confirmed our Monday date, I let him take the lead in regards to our plans, because I think that's the job of the person doing the asking out, which was still technically him, training wheels or not. So, with equal parts optimism, horniness, and plain old being a dum-dum-ness, I took the train into the belly of the beast. By the way, remember the nice things about dogs and chocolate I said about Brooklyn before? None of them apply to Williamsburg. Fuck Williamsburg. I hope it sinks into the East River.

I WALKED up the subway stairs and saw Jonathan across North Sixth Street. He was way shorter than I expected him or any nonmidget to be, but otherwise very cute. I wore heels that night, and a dress, like an adult on a date. He wore corduroys and Vans sneakers, and crossed the street to give me a hug, with a hop in his gait like the top half of a bobblehead doll. We walked down Bedford Avenue together, me hovering over his shaggy blond head.

I found out soon enough that our agenda for the evening was as low-key as the "ace" indoor or outdoor hello he'd initially proposed. Jonathan took me for a walk around his neighborhood, which, I figured out soon enough, was the main activity of the night. I'm always suspicious when a guy takes his date on a walk, because it reeks of poverty and an inability to plan. Soon, we passed a rock club I said I was curious about since it moved to its new location, even though I wasn't, and was just making conversation. Jewish girls, so you know, are terrified of silence. Jonathan asked if I wanted to see the inside of the club.

"Sure," I lied. "That would be *fun*."

The club owner, as it turned out, was a big fan of Jonathan's band. He fell over himself to impress my date, avoiding eye contact with me like it was some kind of endurance challenge reverse staring contest. We got a VIP tour of the place, and spent what seemed like hours touring the club dressing rooms, soundboard, coatroom, even the toilets, while the owner barfed music gossip at Jonathan and pressured him for details about his new album. Jonathan amicably soaked it all in, smiling, nodding, easy-breezy, all lowercase. He was "chill," which is a noun that dicks have recently made into an adjective.

After the tour, we walked around his neighborhood some more, where he ran into so many people he knew, I thought they were plants to impress me. It was like he was taking me for a stroll on his estate—and from the way people on the street reacted to him, it seemed that he was, at least in his mind, the prince of Williamsburg.

"Hey, Jonathan! How's the album going?"

"Oh hi, Jonathan! When did you get back from Seattle?"

"Jonathan! Is the album done? When are you touring?"

Jonathan and I wound up in a bar, where we sat next to each other on stools. There were more people he knew inside: his downstairs roommate, who worked at the bookstore that became a cheese shop, and her girlfriend, who gardened. The colloquial incestuousness turned me off, maybe because I felt left out and maybe because I felt like his attention was so diffused that I'd be lucky to get any time alone with him at all. He seemed to be dating the whole neighborhood, and I was just another extra on The Jonathan Show.

When I got my beer, he finally turned away from his friends, and then he put his knee in between my legs, and I remembered why I'd agreed to go out with him in the first place. I felt my contempt for his Peter Pan posturing slip away as hormones took my body hostage. Suddenly, all I could think about was how the corduroy over his knee felt in between my bare thighs.

He told me he'd bought a DVD of *The Electric Company* to show episodes to his son, because he knew I was a fan of 1970s children's television.

"Do you wanna come over and watch *The Electric Company*?" I squeezed his knee with my legs.

"Sure."

JONATHAN LIVED in a one-bedroom apartment, and converted the bedroom into a playroom for his little boy. It was cluttered with wooden toys, and everything was at shin-level; he kept it that way for whenever his kid came to visit him, which seemed to be not very often.

We retired to the living room, where dresser drawers hid a Murphy bed. His mattress lowered like a drawbridge, and we kissed until I was naked. We made out for a few hours: it was fine, clumsy fun. I had him leave the lights on, so I could watch him, and then I had him call me a car service so I could sleep in my own bed when it was over.

"How did it go?" Nate asked me the next day. I told him everything.

"It doesn't seem like you *like* him," Nate said.

"But he was so cute!" I replied.

Jonathan texted me three days later.

"hope you got home okay last night i had fun!"

Then, right afterward, "oops sorry julie i thought i sent that text tuesday."

Oh, technology. Thanks to you, there are so many more ways to fail.

After the fail text, I didn't hear anything from Jonathan for a couple of weeks, which was disappointing. I feel dumb admitting it, especially after Nate had pointed out that I didn't even like him, but I guess I thought a face-to-face encounter might encourage him to launch into action mode. I'm not the first woman under the impression that her magical vagina will inspire a man to change.

A FEW weeks later, I took a trip to Chicago, where I had a close encounter with a good-looking drummer with broad shoulders who took me back to his place on the South Side, but didn't make a move. He was taking care of his ex's ancient, dying lapdog while she was on tour, because she was, of course, also a rock musician. I remember thinking he was taking me home with him under the guise of "feeding the dog," but that he, in fact, would be sexing me big-time within moments of entering his place. Instead, I came in to find a decrepit, rodent-like creature shedding into a dirty towel in front of the TV, which blasted *Emeril* for its benefit when no one was home.

The drummer stroked that sad animal's head, and I realized he was conflicted between wanting to screw the willing out-of-towner and being stuck in a flailing relationship with his ex, embodied by that sick little dog. I ended up going back to my hotel that night frustrated and horny out of my mind, not to mention having cast another strike against musicians, and the next thing I knew, I was texting Jonathan from JFK, having spent the entire flight back home thinking about degrading sexual acts I had been cheated out of by a shih tzu mix. I asked Jonathan if he was around later. My intention was not "Maybe

I was wrong about this guy." It was "If I don't get laid tonight, I will kill myself."

JONATHAN TEXTED back. He said he was cleaning but that I could come over, and I said I'd bring my copy of the *Free to Be . . . You and Me* special, on the off-chance he was up for some '70s kids' TV, which, by now, I meant as a euphemism. I cabbed over to his place and we hung out in his kitchen listening to records. He offered me ravioli and pot from the stashbox where he kept his coke and rolling papers, while he told me about his son.

The custody proceedings in the past week had gotten ugly, he said, and he was heartbroken about it. I asked him about her. He told me they went out for three months, but that "she was never his girlfriend." After he broke up with her, according to Jonathan, she told him that she was pregnant. He thought she was on the Pill. He called her crazy, a sociopath; getting pregnant so he wouldn't leave her, like that's ever happened before in the history of time. He left anyway, and she ended up having his son and taking the baby with her to Europe, where they spell "neighbor" with a "u."

I listened carefully to Jonathan's story so I could draw my own conclusions. I wondered if that girl wasn't crazy, just dumb and reckless. I felt bad for her if she thought a baby could act as Maturity Miracle-Gro on a man who dated her for months but still kept it casual. But I felt bad for Jonathan, too. His situation was a symptom of a life lived dreamily, while reality charged on. He was sideswiped by this woman's actions; what he thought was her agenda. His idea of plans, after all, was strolling around his neighborhood saying hello to people who sold cheese and grew tulips. He was in over his head with that woman, and maybe that's why he dated girls like me, ten years his junior. I

remember Collette telling me how his songs were about long-
ing and loss. It made sense that the love of Jonathan's life, this
little boy with yellow hair, lived halfway across the world.

Jonathan made sure to use a condom with me that night,
on his son's bed.

I DIDN'T hear from him for three weeks after we slept together,
which was more annoying once I realized I'd left the cute new
earrings I bought in Chicago and my *Free to Be . . . You and Me*
DVD at his apartment. I felt like a fool when I thought about his
baby mama. About his dull songs. But above all, I was just bit-
ter from the experience of spending the night with a guy who
wasn't breaking down my door for seconds. I knew I was making
a mistake when I agreed to go out with Jonathan, I just wanted it
to be a fun mistake. And now I felt bad, and I felt bad for feeling
bad, too, because I knew he was a flake from the start.

If he didn't have my stuff, I wouldn't have gotten in
touch with him. The whole thing would have vaporized and I
would've told myself not to date a musician again. And maybe
I would have anyway, but as it turns out, I haven't. Either way,
I knew that he wasn't going to call; I was waiting for the Great
Pumpkin to give me back my earrings. I decided to end it that
night, if only for the sake of getting my stuff back.

I sent Jonathan a curt text on my way to the L train, telling
him I'd be in his neighborhood later. In the meantime, I had
drinks with a friend at a bar on Lorimer, and finally heard back
from him five hours after I told him I wanted my stuff.

"hi julie. so sorry i've been out of touch. things have been
crazy. the other thing is that i've started seeing somebody. anyway, i have your stuff, just let me know where i can drop it off,
xo jonathan."

I got so angry. How did this happen? I wasn't some groupie. He approached *me*. I may not have been as dumb as the girl who let him knock her up, but I was still a moron, proceeding with something that had "Warning—Don't" all over it. I felt myself get jealous, not of the girl he was now "seeing," but of him, for having so many suckers to breeze through at his princely leisure. I was mad at him for being so lame and mad at myself for getting myself into what was now an awkward mess, with feelings and everything. Even though I saw right through this clown, I still managed to get hurt. It wasn't fair.

I ignored more texts from Jonathan asking me the exact address of the bar where I told him I was, one saying he Googled it, never mind, and one chirping "on the way!" Then I saw him enter the place, holding a shopping bag. He saw me sitting with my friend, and slid into the booth next to us. The awkwardness was palpable. Why did he sit down? Did he really think this was an opportunity to socialize and make nice? Catch up? Chat? Flirt? Just like he thought I lived near him: did he honestly assume that I was as low-key, as lowercase, as he was, about what had happened? That we'd be *friends* now? I guess my policy about who I'm friends with is stricter than the one about who I sleep with, because I can't be friends with somebody unless I actually like them.

He said hi, like a cheerful idiot who didn't know there was something wrong, and gave me the shopping bag with my stuff in it. I thanked him absently and stared at my drink, hoping he'd get the hint to go and fuck off. Then there was a long, obscene silent pause: the kind that makes Jewish girls wish somebody was scratching a blackboard instead, just to fill the space.

"So," Jonathan said, turning to me, grinning like a golden boy. "What are you doin'?"

I took in a sharp breath. "Having a *drink*," I said, answering the world's stupidest question.

My friend smiled nervously and looked down at the floor. Jonathan took a moment to add it up. Nobody was looking at the star of The Jonathan Show. He noticed for the first time that I was glaring down at my drink and not at him. He saw my friend blushing and cringing. And, I like to think, maybe he saw that he made a mistake of his own, thinking his charm would let him weasel out unscathed from what had become an uncomfortable affair.

After a few more pregnant seconds, Jonathan silently got up from the booth and skulked out of the bar into the night.

I took out my DVD and put on my earrings. I crumpled up the shopping bag he used to carry them, and then I finished my Diet Coke.

so you want to date a musician

At some point, learning how to play the guitar, for men, has become a rite of passage in line with shooting a deer, or losing your virginity to a prostitute on your dad's dime. It's what guys learn how to do so they can get laid—because it works. Ask that guy from the Counting Crows! He's awful and he's *still* always knee-deep in muff.

Meanwhile, crushing on musicians is a phase most straight girls go through, and some never get over. My rock-star phase lasted through high school and college. I saw a ton of live shows, and when the singer was cute enough, I hit on that moldy observation that the expression on a guy's face when he's playing guitar is similar to the one on his face when he's totally doing you. But it's harder to date a musician in real life than it is to pretend that a good-looking guy is getting off from sex with you, instead of just trying to remember how the bridge goes.

Here are a couple of things you need to know if you want to go out with a guy who plays music.

First of all, you have to remember that you'll never be able to compete with his bandmates. Remember all that "Yoko" mythology? How these four beautiful boys—even Ringo, if he was lit correctly in 1967—supposedly lived harmoniously and created silky sounds until one of them dared love a woman who made *conceptual art*? What a dumb bit of cultural detritus—that Yoko broke up the Beatles—and, on top of it, what an offensive phrase: "My band *broke up*." You can't marry your band, even in Maine. But if you're going to be a musician's girlfriend, you have to know that your man will always love his bandmates in a way you can't even touch, because they are the guys who help him create *music*. You can only help him create a living human being, with your dumb uterus.

The other thing you should get used to if you're involved with a musician is that you're expected to go to every gig of his that you can. And he could have a show at times of the week during which no sensible human being would leave her apartment. Even Sunday night, which everybody knows is for Chinese food and HBO. It is not for putting on stockings and makeup so you can watch four people you'd have nothing to say to individually over dinner slam out eight songs after making you wait for an hour while they set up equipment.

So much about live rock shows is insufferably boring. The unfunny patter. The awkward dancing the singer will do to "get into it" even though sometimes there are more people onstage than in the crowd. The standing around. The expensive drinks. The sound of it all being so loud that you can't chat with the poor friend you dragged along to see them. All you can do is stand and watch the band play, which doesn't even make sense because there's nothing to *watch*. It's not Laser Floyd, and there is usually no choreography.

But you have to go to the show if you're sleeping with the guy who's playing. You have to be supportive, and stand back after their set, during his postmortem with his bandmates, half-listening to them tell one another "Good show, man!" and then you have to tell him the same thing, and pretend you like hanging out after the show with his friends.

I do not mean to disparage music. I am most definitely *in favor of music*, which you have to be, or else you're not totally human. Just like you have to have a sense of humor, which is why most dancers aren't fully human, despite what their amazing bodies belie. But being guilted into going to go see rock shows in my twenties felt like being dragged to a museum when I was a kid. And not the fun kind of museum, where you can touch stuff, and pretend you're snot, and climb around a giant nose.

But nobody validates you! Everybody loves going to rock shows. Somebody will tell you "I got tickets for Girl Talk" and you have to say something like, "Wow!" or "I'm jealous!" even though you're thanking God you don't have to endure whatever that is exactly.

I remember the first time I realized I didn't like indie rock—it was like I had taken my first deep breath. I felt like Lily Tomlin as Rose Shelton in *Big Business* when she realizes she doesn't belong in Manhattan. "I hate New York in June!" she exclaims to Fred Ward, who was all too happy to take her back home to Jupiter Hollow and lavish one of America's comeliest lesbian comediennes with the spoils of his redneck erection.

My advice to women who habitually gravitate toward musicians is that they learn how to play an instrument and start making music themselves. Not only will they see that it's not that hard, but sometimes I think women just want to be the very thing they think they want to sleep with. Because if you're bright enough—no offense, Tawny Kitaen—sleeping with a musician probably won't be enough for you to feel good about yourself. Even if he writes you a song for your birthday. Don't you know that a musician who writes a song for you is like a baker you're dating making you a cake? Aim higher.

And this goes for women who've just gotten out of a relationship—but more likely a "situation"—with any creative guy; not just a musician. The supportive ones who were involved with an improv comedian who had to stomach his troupe's shows. The ladies who had to read the scripts and short stories their aspiring writer boyfriends sent to their work e-mail and give generous notes and way-too-kind feedback on the terrible story arc or the cringe-inducing dialogue, thinking, "I can do better than that" and "This is embarrassing."

But most importantly, even when you're in the throes of an affair with a guy whose rock-star confidence made you melt in the first place, don't forget that it's you who's the star. A successful relationship with any guy is going to ground itself in him knowing that he shines, but you shine brighter, and the two of you together are unstoppable. Because it's about him deserving you, not choosing you at random from a harem of devotees.

And if you're the one at the lip of the stage hoping to get perspired on or clamoring for an autograph, that doesn't speak too well of your own inherent desirability. You're sort of putting him in a feminine role up there, watching him decked out in eyeliner, singing a song, aren't you? Remember: before there were groupies, there were stage-door suitors—guys who'd wait outside the dressing rooms of chorus girls with diamonds, sweating bullets.

Follow what it is that you love and makes you want to be better, always. But don't get yourself tied up with any kind of rock star—musician or not—who makes you feel like you're not made of star stuff. Because of course you are. Give me a break.

the kid

I was running late for my date with Noah, so I texted him.

"Hi! Sorry I'm running late. Can we say 9:45 instead of 9? I'm coming in from North Brunswick, New Jersey (DON'T ASK), and apparently NJ Transit likes to make up their train schedule as they go along."

I was coming from a Memorial Day barbeque hosted by a couple of friends, one of whom dropped me off at the New Brunswick station a full hour before the train came.

Noah was an aspiring writer, so his texts were clever and impeccably punctuated. "No problem," he wrote back. "But just know that, when you arrive, I will grill you mercilessly about what you were doing in North Brunswick."

We met at a bar in his neighborhood for our lager date, which was supposed to have been dinner, but ended up being us drinking pints of beer after I got into the city late. I arrived to find Noah at the bar drinking solo, and my first impression of him was that he was the youngest person I'd ever seen inside of a bar. Drinking that beer made him look very "I learned it from you, Dad! I learned it by watching *you!*"

I'd met, or at least seen Noah in passing from the proverbial "around," and we'd sent each other a few e-mails after a mutual friend introduced us at a show, but I didn't remember him being quite so castable as apple-cheeked pedo bait on *To Catch a Predator*. I mean, he really looked like a teenage boy, and it was disconcerting. I tried hard to act normal, and he cracked a ton of jokes, and after a few beers, all was fine, as it tends to be.

I don't usually drink beer, and if I do, I'll pull at a bottle of Amstel like it's an exotic liqueur. So because I was downing pint after pint like I was a British guy who liked soccer, it meant that I was going to be drunk soon with a boy who looked fourteen.

Meanwhile, Noah gave me his spiel—he told me that he'd gone to Harvard and he detailed his career ambitions. I soaked up his optimism like a cynical sponge and chimed in whenever I had a nasty thing to say about one of the people he talked about whom we both knew, because that's what I think flirting is.

Noah was twenty-six, it turned out. And while I was just twenty-nine, I felt like I was picking up a middle-schooler from his karate lesson to get him home in time for dinner. He had the looks of a farm boy, complete with his strawlike bowl haircut and baby-fat face and bad jeans that he picked out himself once he left home for Cambridge. But what made Noah seem even younger was his boundless enthusiasm.

It must be a symptom of Ivy Leaguers who haven't yet

had their dreams crushed to broadcast their ambitions cockily. They are kids who've never been told "no," who figure that the odds—and in the world of *showbiz* no less—were competitive, sure, but not for *them*. They knew from competitive: They got into those schools, right? They figured that the rest of their lives would be a cake walk. I don't actively dislike Ivy League grads as much as the people who complain that Harvard brats suck up all the good jobs that nepotism doesn't, but the cluck on this chick got on my nerves only because I'd been at the same game as him for what seemed like ages longer, and it's *tough*, you guys. For those of you considering starting a career in entertainment, don't! It's the worst! They make you eat shit and you have to pretend you like it! That you like eating shit! Only dogs like eating shit, and that's a bad example, because dogs are the best! Anyway, showbiz stinks and life is hard. But Noah didn't seem to have wind of obstacle one.

He told me about a pilot he was writing, and about an agent he'd been introduced to, who was, at the time, the same agent I'd been working with. I told him that I'd put in a good word on his behalf, which seemed like a sucker move even as I heard the words leave my mouth. He thanked me, and I felt like his advisor. He told me about his actual mentors—all his former professors from Harvard invested in his postcollegiate success. I drank faster and narrowed my eyes, like Patsy on *Ab Fab*, wondering how talented this kid actually was. That's one of the pitfalls of dating within your industry: Flirting turns into shop talk really fast, and then you're competing, which is not a turn-on for me at all.

WE TOOK a walk when we were done with all that beer, and ended up near his place. Noah invited me up to his apartment with the exertion of a kid using every resource he'd been born with to seem casual. His voice sprung up at the end of his offer, like a curlicue. I said yes, and Junior chirped in with his eager soprano: "Cool!"

I decided that we would only make out as I ascended the front stoop of a venerable brownstone in Chelsea. What would have been a lovely old pre-war apartment was sullied by the fact that Noah shared his place with four other young guys who'd just graduated from college, so the place was predictably dormlike and filthy. While Noah peed, I perused his DVDs, which were displayed in the "common area" alongside his roommates' standard college-age titles in one of those media racks you see at Best Buy. When he came out of the bathroom he told me to "pick a movie," and I promptly did not. I don't like assignments when I'm being hosted, whether it's "Take off your shoes" or "Choose from *Pulp Fiction*, *Spaceballs*, or *The Big Lebowski* as the movie we're going to watch for five minutes before we start frenching."

I told Noah that I'd rather watch the movie he spent a lot of time at the bar telling me about, but he only had it on his computer, which he kept in his bedroom, which was a relief, because the "common area"/living room was giving me a big case of the sads.

We sat next to each other atop the loft bed that he told me, pridefully, he built from scratch himself, like the famous carpenter, Jesus Christ, and he hit PLAY on the Quicktime file or whatever, then put his hand on my thigh. I surveyed the offerings of his tiny bedroom and found it just below my modest expectations of how a straight guy in his twenties might live with four other dudes exactly like him. There was the Ikea desk, copies of Woody Allen's prose in milk crates, and tiny closets packed with sprawling, unfolded clothes nestled behind hung sheets in lieu of proper doors. A pigeon nested over the air conditioner that was wedged inside his tiny window, which lent us a view into a grubby alley. Dorm Life Forever, I guess. Thirty seconds into the opening credits of the movie, Noah attacked my mouth with his tongue.

I DON'T usually date younger guys, so I was taken aback by what I assume was age-appropriate Golden Retriever–like enthusiasm when Noah knocked me down with tongue-based affection. His eagerness, which I'd found annoying when he spoke of his career goals, was all of a sudden an asset to the action. He dove into my crotch and slurped at my groin like there was sap inside my womb he was tapping for pancake syrup, and I was impressed at the strength that came from what I'd assumed was a modest frame.

We made out for a while, rolling around athletically and smooching like robust teenagers. And then I fell off the bed.

I fell like a rock, too, and from the loft's considerable height. There was a thump and everything. It really hurt. I still have a scar on my lower back from the impact of whatever prewar nail or screw dealie awaited my sacrum on the floorboard below Noah's handcrafted Loft Bed of Doom.

"Oof," I said.

Noah didn't miss a beat. He helped me up and kept fooling around with me, so there was no break in our make-out momentum. This is what twenty-six-year-old boys do when they have erections. Nothing gets in their way. I didn't know how to react—I was still smarting from my fall. But then Noah took off his shirt, and I had a cougar-at-Chippendales moment when I saw his bare chest.

I forgot my lower back pain instantly, and all of a sudden, remembered Noah's offhand remark at the bar about how he went to the gym every day before work. It was an anomaly among his otherwise typical slovenly comedy writer traits—his bathroom was dirty, his clothes were sloppy, and his bedroom pulled off that uniquely young male feat of being at once stark and messy at the same time. Back to his upper body, though. It is the star of this story.

Noah's chest was V-shaped and adorned with a stippled hair pattern. There were muscles—not the veiny kind either—and the whole thing rippled hypnotically, like a 3-D Magic Eye drawing from the 1990s, though that may have been the fall affecting the equilibrium section of my brain. It was the Greatest Torso I'd Ever Seen—I wanted to give it a round of applause. We forgot about me falling, and kept making out until I had to pee, trudging bravely out into the hallway toward his gross bathroom. I washed my hands obsessively, then looked into the mirror. Enough time had passed and enough booze had worn off: I was then on the brink of what would be a *decision*.

I rejoined Noah on his dangerous bed to let him know that I thought it would be a good idea for me to go home. I figured we'd reached the point of no return in the make-out department, and were either going to get each other sloppily off, or I would leave like a lady, or at least somebody with the willpower to get herself back home after second base and regular third, sort of, over the pants.

I was very proud of myself for deciding to establish my boundaries. What a treat for us both! I'd leave him wanting more *and* get to make up for what I'd worried was an inappropriately early return to a gent's boudoir without dinner and such. And it was our first date, besides. I was so proud of myself, like I was getting ready to order a salad at the pizza place. I returned to the bedroom and told Noah what I'd decided. I explained to him that I had to get up early and couldn't stay, and he said he understood.

And then he bent me over the side of his bed and fucked me from behind.

YES, THAT bed. It was so high that my feet dangled an inch off the floor, but Noah, bless his mid-twenties determination, still managed to get behind and inside of me, and pounded for what seemed like a good forty-five seconds, muttering the whole time to me, the pigeon outside, and the abstract pattern-morphing screen saver on the laptop turned toward the bed:

"Is this what you wanted? Is it?"

And maybe it was. I guess I wasn't sure. But once it was happening, I was OK with it. I mean, it didn't *feel* good. I'm not a reticent rape victim or anything: It was consensual like a fox—and conceptually exciting, I suppose. The kind of action you settle for in high school because you're not used to having an orgasm, and the youth of your inexperienced partner is not unique. It was actually *funny*, the abrupt timing of it all, after my weak protests. Maybe I could recommend his writerly instincts to my agent with more confidence than I had earlier in the evening.

Afterward, I took a moment to think about what to do. I'd been getting ready to pack up and head home moments before, but then, there had been sex. I figured, "Well, now, I *have* to sleep over, because if I *don't*, then I'm a huge slut."

So I did. And in the morning, when I got up to brush my

teeth with my finger, Noah's bathroom door opened with the sound of a flush, revealing a shirtless *dude* in his twenties with a half-up/half-down ponytailed hairstyle. I was taken aback: I usually don't see anybody that early in the morning, and because I don't live in Tampa, I never see hair like that.

"Oh, that's Doug. He's an investment banker/body builder," Noah explained to me once I told him who I'd met. And of course it was. Of course it was Doug. I had to get out of there before I met more of his roommates with career/hobby hybrids. I slipped on the summer dress and jacket I'd had on in the bar ten hours earlier and raced home so I could take a shower. I felt sort of gross.

It wasn't until I was back in my apartment when I realized how itchy and irritated my skin was. There were bites all over my legs and under my arms, and my eyes were red even after I showered. I looked more closely at the bites, and my heart sank.

Fucking bedbugs.

SLEEPING WITH Noah exposed me to the trendiest and most notorious of New York City's formidable vermin population. He had given me the real estate form of an STD. I went to bedbugger.com and studied examples of the bites I was certain came from that stupid fucking bed Noah sawed and nailed together with plywood and capped with a mattress that probably came from the street. I pictured his cotton dorm room comforter and his flannel sheets. I remembered the pigeon's nest outside his window; rats with wings defecating over the A/C. The filthy pre-war walls, mauve with lead paint. That bathroom. I took another shower and made an emergency appointment with my dermatologist, a nice man.

I started seeing Dr. Steingart a while ago, when I called the office of Dr. Nussbaum—the 9/11 herpes informant—to find out that he had died of old age. "I'm sorry to hear that. When can I come in to get this acne scraped?" I asked the grieving receptionist at the time.

Seven years later, after spending the night with Noah, I waited for Dr. Steingart to look at my bites while my favorite of his nurses made small talk with me, as she always does, about her favorite stand-up comedians, all of whom are black. Barbara is a tiny Italian American woman who lives in New Rochelle and has worked as a nurse, seemingly, since the beginning of time. The only thing she likes more than reprimanding me for picking at a zit is telling me how much she loves Sinbad. It was comforting to hear her voice that afternoon: Barbara was suddenly the only person I wanted to be around that day, in the aftermath of an evening plagued with vermin bites and intercourse absent of clitoral stimulation.

When she asked what the reason was for my seeing Dr. Steingart that day, I told Barbara that I'd slept in a guy's bed the night before and was convinced I was pecked to death by the bugs that dwelled in its crevices. She told me the doctor would be right in, and also, how much she was looking forward to seeing Steve Harvey at Mohegan Sun the following weekend. And soon enough, there was Dr. Alvin Steingart to look at my bites, shake his head, and remind me that I should be careful about whose bed I sleep in.

I felt like I did in college, going to the gynecologist for confessionlike absolution after each one of my sexual misdoings. Even though Noah and I used a condom, the Xeroxed *New York Post* article about the bedbug epidemic Dr. Steingart handed me was a black-and-white reminder that there are still sticky wickets besides chlamydia, to circumnavigate after the deed.

AND OF *course* I should have been more careful about whose bed I slept in. Because there are so many complications that come from sex you assume is casual and non-reoccurring—the "failed pilot" kind of sex. If something bad happens after what turns out to be a one-night stand, from heartache to bedbug bites, there's an excellent chance you won't feel comfortable contacting your one-time partner to report the somber findings, unless they are life-threatening and you're at a genuine moral crossroads. But if you're entertaining the idea of maybe seeing him again, and nobody has any oozing sores, part of you is still compelled to stay mute, because we've been indoctrinated by people who make the rules about how a girl who wants another date should *keep it light.*

Women, even when plagued with problems that transcend wanting to be liked by a cute boy, are still under the impression that you shouldn't contact a guy after he schtupps you, especially the day after, even as you're writing a check out to your dermatologist because *nobody fucking takes Freelancers Union Insurance.* But you don't send the guy the bill, even though you're tempted to, because you're wise enough to know that as soon as you've consented to sex of any kind, no matter what you hope comes of it, as soon as it's over, you're back in the business of taking care of yourself.

SO I sealed off the clothes I'd worn the night before in a Ziploc freezer bag and sent the whole mess to the cleaners, and after I cleaned my place like a Stepford Wife on the diet pills they used to make that had cocaine in them, I took a third shower and changed my sheets. And then I was done.

As far as ailments go, I was relieved to have come down with the kind of sick that can be treated with some Cortisone cream and good apartment hygiene. And I was disappointed that Noah never followed through on his e-mails after that night to get together again, after what I'd had all intentions to be a proper date. I felt like I blew it by coming home with him in the first place, but I guess it was good to have Noah's failed test of interest up front, so I didn't waste more time wondering whether he was a long-term contender.

But it still hurt to see him shift from caring enough to impress me with cute texts to ignoring my e-mail about the Nicolas Cage movie that came on late at night—the one we were talking about back at the bar. I blamed myself, but who knows if anyone besides the bugs were actually culpable. In the end, I made a clean break, and didn't carry Noah into my thoughts any more than I carried vermin into my apartment. Sometimes you have to be your own preemptive exterminator.

did i come to brooklyn for this?

I substitute-taught a class one time and ended up going out with one of my students. It was a writing class—for *adults*, so calm down—and one of the students was a really good-looking guy in his late thirties. He was wearing a button-down plaid shirt and had a generous smile, and as soon as I saw him, I thought to myself, "Hello."

One of the things I do when I teach a class, whether it's my first session or when I sub and I'm teaching a bunch of people I don't know, is go around the room and have everybody introduce themselves. It's a good frame of reference for me so I know what people's backgrounds are, and everybody likes talking about themselves. Plus I get to engage in a conversationlike experience, which is the best part of teaching—when you feel like you're not actually working.

So, we went around the room and my students for the day

gave me their bios. A middle-aged woman with eager eyes who half-smiled at everything I said, like she hoped I was about to say something funny so she could laugh, told me about her former broadcast journalism career and subsequent divorce. A heavy blonde in her early twenties said she just graduated from the New School, where she majored in creative writing. A bona fide freak—there is always at least one in any adult education class in New York City, God bless and keep them, rambled on about Bush's war on terror, Monty Python, how he lived in the housing complex on Twenty-fifth Street and Eighth Avenue, and how if it weren't for his Latin neighbor's loud macaw, he'd be able to concentrate on drawing his own political cartoons. And then, Alistair, the cute guy with the plaid shirt, said he worked at AOL as his day job, that he was an artist when he lived in Austin, Texas, and that since he moved to New York, wanted to do more writing.

And that was, frankly, enough for me to know to decide I wanted to go out with Alistair. He was cute, and he could string a sentence together. That was literally it. It wasn't like I heard "Austin . . . AOL . . . Art . . ." and decided "Yes!" It was more like "Sure. Fine. He's not unemployed. Maybe he's normal." It is an optimistic assumption we all have about good-looking people.

Alistair may have been able to speak lucidly, but the piece he wrote for the class, however, was absolutely incomprehensible. It wasn't that it was *bad*—though I guess it was that, too. It just didn't make any sense at all. It was a sketch that took place at a Senate hearing, and the premise of the whole thing was based on this really obscure FAA motion that had gone out the week before, and all the FAA chairmen were shouting at the senators, but not about anything I could understand. And there weren't any jokes in it. Maybe there were lines in it that he *thought* were jokes, but it was all pretty cryptic. But sadly, at that point I didn't really care how good of a writer he was. I just wanted to go on a date with him and maybe make out.

I FOUND Alistair on Facebook and asked our mutual friends about him, and he got decent marks, so I wrote him and asked if he wanted to go to a show we'd talked about after class, during which I was certain we were flirting. "I can't," he wrote back, "I have a girlfriend. . . . I mean plans." Then he used an emoticon—a sideways sticking-its-tongue-out smiley face. He continued. "Sorry, I don't mean to be presumptuous. I just find you really attractive, and wanted to be as upfront as I could. And I don't think going out with you would be the best idea under those circumstances."

Adorable! I mean, I was disappointed, but I was also positively tickled at how Alistair showed me his hand. "Here's my deal, here's what I'm saying, here's why I'm saying it." That's what *I* do! I'm totally transparent and excessively forthcoming too!

Here's the difference, though: I'm not crazy. Alistair was, which is something I should have known right away from the writing he brought to class. At first I just wondered if he was just not very bright. There were some inexcusable spelling mistakes in his piece, and not of the "you're/your" variety. Plus, like I said, the content of his scene was totally bats. But handsome passes for normal and intelligent when you decide you want it to.

I wrote back to Alistair, thanking him for being honest, and moved on with my life, only to hear from him six weeks later. He asked me out, and when I asked, "Wouldn't your girlfriend mind?" He wrote back and told me that they'd gone their separate ways. That was fast! We made a date for Saturday night: I told him I wanted to see the new Indiana Jones movie.

That was another premonition of bad things to come. *Indiana Jones and the Kingdom of the Crystal Skull* is not only the worst movie of the *Indiana Jones* franchise, surpassing the one where they eat brains out of monkey skulls and there's an "Oriental Little Boy," but it's also, quite possibly, the worst movie of all time. There are aliens, mind control, Russians, Shia LaBeouf playing a character called "Mutt," and it makes no sense at all. It made Alistair's sketch for class look like *Lawrence of Arabia*.

Alistair didn't understand why seeing that movie caused me to become psychotic. He thought it was all right, but wasn't overly familiar with the other *Indiana Jones* films, which seemed odd, considering he was roughly my age and male. I had a hard time connecting with him over the abomination we'd just sat through, and so I changed the subject over the course of our walk to a restaurant.

That was when Alistair told me about how much he was looking forward to going back to Burning Man that summer. And *that* was the moment when I figured that in terms of us not having anything in common, it couldn't get worse.

DON'T YOU love that expression? "How could this get worse?" If ever there was a transitional phrase that better telegrapheds a bit of storytelling, I'd like to know what it is. You're planting a red flag into the ground, and printed on that flag is, SOMETHING HORRIBLE IS ABOUT TO HAPPEN. What could be a more obvious foreshadowing device? "Well, at least it's not raining?"

So, we're at this Mexican restaurant. And over chips, Alistair, whose candor I'd found endearing in his e-mails about how attractive he found me, quickly lent itself to a *Hall of Presidents–*

style illumination of all of his skeletons, which any half-sane person with the social skills of a high-functioning idiot savant would have had the foresight to know belonged safely tucked away behind psychological winter coats and formalwear in the hall closets of our minds. He simply did not know what to keep to himself on a first date.

He told me at length about his ex-girlfriend; that they met after spending a weekend together when one of his friends married her sister. After that, she went back to Cyprus, where she was from, obviously. And after a month of long distance flirting, Athena or whatever quit her job and broke up with her boyfriend in order to move to the States into Alistair's apartment, and then, within two months, acquired a pretty serious Vicodin habit after she had his abortion. So there was that.

It was a whirlwind romance, contained in a few months and told to me in the time it took for our enchiladas to arrive. I was almost impressed by how cracked this guy had to be, not only to live this reality, but to relay it with such ease to a first date—with no sense of shame or decorum at all. What a disaster was Alistair. It was like he was the living personification of *Indiana Jones and the Kingdom of the Crystal Skull*.

Then he told me about the time he was arrested.

He was living in Portland, Oregon, at the time, so I figured he wasn't incarcerated for any kind of offense that wasn't adorable. I've never been to the Pacific Northwest, but my impression of that part of the country is that it's all café au laits and ironic lunch boxes. I figured he was arrested for shoplifting one of those Ugly Dolls, or a box of those Band-Aids shaped like bacon strips from one of their hipster gift shops. But then he gave me more data to add to the "Crazy or Stupid?" bar graph poll in my mind—the one that was quickly becoming a Venn diagram with a lot of overlap. Alistair told me that he used to "party" a lot, which explained the impulse control he failed to exercise with the Cypriot, not to mention the cranberry juice and soda he ordered with his meal, and soon I was treated to the story that narrated his push into the twelve-stepiverse.

He was wasted one night, which is a great way to start an "I got arrested" story, because you know already that the point isn't how he *got* that way but what he did once he was. It was around four a.m., and wasted Alistair saw a car idling, its doors open and nobody in the front seat, in a Chevron Food Mart parking lot, where he ended up alone, though he did not remember how or why. At the time, because he was drunk, Alistair thought it would be really *funny* to drive around in that idling car. The one that wasn't his. That's what he thought would be funny. I thought about the sketch he'd brought to class before, and wondered if indeed there *were* jokes in it—only they were "Alistair Jokes."

So, he's drunk and high on something too, and he's taking this late-night joy ride in a stranger's sedan at a high speed around Portland, when he suddenly realizes he's being followed by a heap of squad cars. And then, once he sees their flashing lights in his rearview mirror, he also catches sight of what's in the backseat of the car. He turns around to confirm what he saw, still speeding on the evergreen, drizzly streets of Oregon, and there it is: a toddler, asleep in a baby seat. In the car he ostensibly stole.

Long, dreadful, horrifying, damning, humiliating short? He was charged with DUI, Grand Theft, and Kidnapping. Funny, right?

I was still processing the news of the Cyprus girl's abortion.

★   ★   ★

BY NOW our dinner was over, and Alistair wanted to go to a bar to have a coffee, which is what alcoholics in recovery drink when they go to bars. So we did, and then he wanted me to come home with him. And you'd think I'd be in the "no way" zone, but, frankly, I was still in the "whatever" zone with this guy, who was clearly a hot mess in so many new and hilarious ways, but also inarguably cute. And besides, I'd already come out to Brooklyn to make out, and frankly, no disrespect to Deana Carter, but "Did I Come to Brooklyn for This?" is the new "Did I Shave My Legs for This?"

A cab took us to an unidentifiable, nightmarish section of what I was told was Prospect Heights, but looked like the set of *The Warriors*. There was a Chevron Food Mart across the street from him, and I didn't even know there were any Chevron Stations in New York City. I guess he managed to find one out of the nostalgia he felt for the hilarious night he stole that car.

He had a second-floor walk-up apartment—a railroad, in the confines of which I felt distinctively unsafe. There was no style to the place—he had hunter-green "teenage boy" tinted walls and a black leather loveseat behind a Target coffee table. I have to say, though—the novelty of going into other people's apartments never gets old for me. Having sex with people is a great way to see what kind of furniture guys have and how their apartments are decorated. It's replaced babysitting for me as the best way to snoop around people's homes.

We made out, and I'd say it was OK, but I honestly don't remember, which probably means it was fine. And we kept going, not because I was turned on, but because it was so dull that I felt the need to step it up, just for the sake of getting the bang for the buck. Like when the food is bland and not so tasty, you just keep stuffing yourself, in hopes that the fullness will substitute for what you're missing. Satiety for flavor swap. Quantity over quality. Lousy food in big portions. You get the idea.

And that's how I found myself on top of Alistair's navy blue cotton comforter, with his dick *and* balls in my mouth. I needed to teabag him out of necessity, because Alistair was the kind of small in which you feel the need to treat his balls like they're part of his penis, just to give the whole situation some extra length. Like when you let somebody keep their shoes on when you're measuring their height. I pretended his balls were the lumpy, wide base of his underwhelming shaft, and he moaned in appreciation over the fat-skinny guy gut he blamed on his breakup with the girl from Cyprus.

We finished, and I had him call me a car service, because there was no way I was going to sleep in that bed, nor was I going to go out and hail a cab in that neighborhood alone any time of day or night. He wrote me the next day and told me he'd had fun, but I saw no point in writing back until my birthday, a few months later, when he reached out to wish me a good one and called me hot stuff, and I let him take me out to dinner again.

That was a bad idea.

I knew it was, as soon as I got a call from him telling me he got lost, even though I gave him excellent directions to a restaurant in Manhattan on the corner of two numbered cross-streets. I'd made the mistake of delegating another evening of my life to this Burning Man festival–attending, pointy dick–having, *Crystal Skull*–liking, self-admitted kidnapper. Still—I'm glad I went. Because after bearing witness to what I'd later call his "Vagina Monologue" at dinner—about how he just isn't sure what he wants to do with his life, whether it's paint or write, and how he thinks he's lazy, maybe, and also has a hard time setting goals for himself because he isn't sure what he wants, and how he doesn't know whether to look for another job or work toward a promotion—I had my answer to the riddle that plagued me since I first met Alistair in my class.

"Is he crazy or stupid or both?" didn't seem to be the most pertinent question anymore with this guy. I had my answer. Alistair was just a loser. Of course he was! Why hadn't I pegged him sooner? I'd made out with enough by then to know one at first glance.

HE WALKED me home after splitting the check, which was lame because the idea was that it was my birthday dinner, and when we got to my building, he asked to come upstairs. I was about to politely refuse, when he begged to use my bathroom. My bathroom! Do people still do that to get laid? "Please, let me come upstairs for sex." No? All right, how about this: "Please let me come upstairs to *move my bowels*." Yeah! That's more like it! Let the boning commence!

So he came upstairs and peed, and then he came out of the bathroom and looked around my apartment. He noticed that I didn't live in a tenement apartment in the "apocalypse" part of Prospect Heights, My Ass, and that my furniture didn't look like it had come from the "Back to College" aisle of a superstore, and, using classic Alistair judgment, he decided he had to comment.

"Wow, what is your rent?" he said. "Like, a million dollars?"

Asking New Yorkers how much rent they pay is like asking someone what she weighs. It is very rude. So at that point,
I made the conscious decision to ignore Alistair, who had officially become a contaminant in my stylish and reasonably
priced Manhattan one-bedroom, and instead of glaring at him
or giggling or responding in any way at all, I silently turned on
the TV.

I flipped through the channels icily as he made his way
next to me on the couch. He put his arm around me and I
didn't move. And soon enough, the small talk about the yogurt
commercials faded into awkward silence, and then he said he
was tired and should go, and I walked him to the door and
decided he stunk.

I got an e-mail from Alistair later that night—a rambling
monologue about how he was sorry for not knowing what
he wanted or something about being more "on it" next time,
and instead of telling him that there was not going to be a
next time or writing back, "That's OK, good to see you!" or
anything else, I deleted the e-mail and forgot about him all
over again. Until the summer, when I saw some photos he
posted on Facebook that he took at Burning Man. He was
in a dress, alongside fellow freaks, behind the wheel of a float
that resembled a giant rubber ducky with a disco ball for a
head.

I took in the scene: the sun, the pink smoke, the sand around
the duck truck that went on for what seemed like miles, the
girls in bikinis and tattoos in giant birdcages on deck. And for
Alistair's sake, I peeked in the back of the float to make sure he
wasn't accidentally transporting a toddler.

red coats and mary wilkies

There's a type of man who stands out when he walks into a room, like the little girl in the red coat from *Schindler's List*. He comes in, and suddenly everyone else around you is black-and-white, offsetting this dynamo, this apple-cheeked, charisma-drenched peacock. That's when you've got to be careful.

I met one of the flashy ones at a reading. The first thing I noticed at the event was him. The second was his wedding band.

I don't, as a general rule, mess around with married men. There are girls who kill themselves over their attention, their duality, their unavailability and empty promises. I slept with one once, when I was traveling in my early twenties, but the experience didn't devastate me because I didn't like the guy very much. He wasn't great in bed, either: He made monkey faces when he moaned and hokey Dad Jokes in between switching positions, and at a certain point he just wanted to talk to me about the TV shows he liked to watch. The only hazard the affair posed to my mental health was my being bored to death. But it still wasn't good for me, and I didn't repeat it.

IF ANYBODY studying psychology wants a concrete example of what a narcissist looks like, I advise them to consider any man who cheats on his wife. These guys are the textbook me-firsters, the ones who think the rules don't apply to them, the ones who tell themselves as long as she doesn't know, there's no harm done. No woman needs to sleep with these guys. There are so many *single* self-absorbed narcissists who will fuck you poorly.

I was downright high on the fumes of my own self-righteous philosophy until Leo walked into that party like he was walking into a Carly Simon song. And Leo taught me in an instant that your convictions about what men should and shouldn't do once they have wives who aren't you is all well and good until someone is flashing this boyish grin at you and undressing you with his eyes and laughing at your jokes and touching your forearm and otherwise being the most charming man you've never met, and you want so badly to be on your back with your panties at your ankles, grinding his face into a soft pulp with your crotch.

All I did was flirt with Leo that night, and he drank it in like a mule at an oasis. Some married men flirt the way starving people pull up to a buffet. They partake of every morsel—each breadstick, every cocktail shrimp; pasta *and* rice—as though it were their last gasp before reboarding the express train of their marriage. Plates are filled; garnish is inhaled. They don't even know what they're doing sometimes; they just know they are so hungry.

The night we met, Leo asked me out to lunch at his work,

and I said yes, and then, he said, "Boy, if I were single . . ." which gave me the chance to mentally finish his trailed-off sentence: ". . . I'd date you *and* fuck you." Leo followed me around the bar that night until Nate came by and sulked, because he was cranky and hungry and didn't want to hang out with writers who dressed terribly at a lousy party, bless him. So Nate and I left to go eat Chinese food, and I came home to an e-mail from Leo, and the correspondences began.

It was a pleasure meeting me, he said, then added, "Who, precisely, was that silent redwood hovering nearby? The guy, I mean. Did I detect a glower?"

He was baiting me, like I'd be dumb enough to play jeal-ousy doubles with a guy who had a spouse to compete with. Maybe he thought he'd luck out negotiating a wife swap. And honestly, for any girl looking to sleep with a Married, the only viable option I can possibly advocate, reporting as a correspon-dent from Crazy Town, is doing it when you're married too. Sometimes that shit works out! Two people in unhappy rela-tionships commiserating as peers? People still get hurt, but at least the low and high status stuff evens out, so it's slightly less unfair than the alternative.

But a single girl dating a married man is begging to be dragged by her hair back into the cave. Because while no man deserves a harem, all of them think they deserve more than one woman to slake their multicompartmentalized male brains. Just because men are able to separate "this one takes care of my children" from "this one does this thing with her bare feet on my taint," it doesn't make it OK for them to multitask once they've committed to being faithful in front of friends and family and an expensive cake.

★　　★　　★

THINK OF all the secretaries in the 1950s and '60s who weren't necessarily married off after high school. They were smart enough to strive toward the workplace, but unable to ascend any merit-based ladder, because of their dumb old vaginas— the ones that may as well have been sandbags. These were the smart girls—like Shirley MacLaine in *The Apartment*—who fell for their peers and had to settle for half their attention, then go back to their apartments and read. Meanwhile, their paramours took the train upstate back home to their wives, once they were done dabbling with their colleagues. They had their cake, and, as Big Edie put it in *Grey Gardens*, "loved it, masticated it, chewed it, and had everything [they] wanted."

I wrote back and I told Leo that Nate wasn't my boy-friend—just a gay guy in a shitty mood, adding, "Though I have been known to pit different kinds of unavailable men against one another for sport."

I'm embarrassed to admit that our e-mails went on for a couple of months after that, because I am weak and because Leo said and did things that guys who were available did not. There were gifts messengered over. Poetry transcribed. He bestowed tons of flattery; about my work, about me being adorable.

WE MADE a date for our lunch at his office, and I picked out a dress. I was turned on all the time then. That's another one of the pitfalls of getting yourself involved with a Married, or even thinking about it; you're distilled down to your purely sexual self, like you're fuck meth. You're not floating around in the glow of being unequivocally loved by the man you want put-ting babies inside of you. You're slinking and bounding across avenues in back-breaking heels, strutting like a pole dancer and choreographing pornography in your head all day.

I changed my mind about our lunch date after I saw *Manhattan* at an outdoor film festival. *Manhattan* is a movie I've seen a thousand times—it's in black and white, like the non-Leo men in the room the night we met. Usually I relate to Mariel Hemingway's character in the movie; the seventeen-year-old who's wiser than all the neurotic adults around her who cheat on one another and sweat minutiae like brownish tap water. She dates Woody Allen's character and gets dumped, and he comes back for her at the end, but it's too late. But when I saw the movie again that summer, it was Diane Keaton's character who made me think of me.

Keaton plays Mary Wilkie, the permed know-it-all from Philadelphia who went to Radcliffe and calls her therapist Donnie. Mary has a dachshund named Waffles and nearly unscalable emotional walls until she concedes to Woody Allen's character one late night at a diner that "he has a good sense of humor," which he didn't need her to tell him. They fall in love after they take a walk and it starts raining and they have to take shelter in the planetarium. But it's complicated because Mary Wilkie is involved with a married man.

"I'm smart, I'm young, I'm beautiful," Mary repeats to an audience of herself, and of course she is, but she also blew her chances with someone who dumped his seventeen-year-old moon-faced girlfriend for her. And it's sad because nobody gets what he or she wants in the end, really, even though they still get to live here; a place whose skyline is scored by *Rhapsody in Blue*.

I didn't want to be Mary Wilkie. And I was no longer seventeen and pie-eyed. I had to write Leo and cancel lunch, even though it killed me to delete the only thing on my calendar I was looking forward to. This is what I said:

While it pains me to bow out, I think it would be best if we didn't get together. I would love to see you, and I have a cute maxi-dress to wear and all of it. But I'm also a recent graduate of the drama-seeking missile years of my twenties, and am trying hard to be wise. The fruits of that particular labor so far include and are not limited to dining with married men I find attractive.

Julie

That was a hard e-mail to write, and most of my motivation for hitting Send was the possibility that he'd only see the last five words of the e-mail and dump his wife. You know, just like that. No big whoop. Like when you have to break up with somebody, but you hope deep down that saying "it's over" is just giving your mess of a boyfriend an obstacle he'll circumnavigate for the reward of being reunited with you, and it feeling so good. But really, you're just saying "This is why this isn't going to work out." You're not asking someone to change so that it can. Because unless you are dealing with a good old-fashioned intervention, with letters family members read out loud and black coffee and sobbing, you can't get somebody to do something they don't decide to do themselves. It is actually ridiculous to think that you can. What's more, a married guy leaving wifey only to settle down with his girl on the side is no sure thing.

RECENTLY, I had drinks with an old friend, Sam, beside whom I used to tend the register at an artsy video rental place back in college, when I was a flirty chubbo with bad taste in clothes, music, and boys (Hawaiian prints, Squirrel Nut Zippers, and avante-garde puppeteers, respectively). Sam was the only guy at the shop who would chat and laugh at my jokes, while my other coworkers would broodingly shelve VHS copies of Truffaut's oeuvre along to Philip Glass music.

When we caught up after I spotted him solo in the audience of one of my shows, Sam told me he'd just separated from his wife of five years in the wake of what he called an "emotional affair" with a woman he worked with at his office. When I asked him to clarify just what the ass that meant, he said that there had been a lot of flirting and e-mailing between the two of them after a business trip they took together, but zero actual hanky panky. His linguistics were baffling. Had I just ended an "emotional affair" with Leo? Or were we just e-mailing? Stupid Marrieds, inventing names for activities they want to lead to actual cheating.

I thought it was at once generous and creepy of Sam to call something like flirty e-mails back and forth an "affair," emotional or otherwise. The word "affair" the way he used it seemed quaint, like an antique political scandal or a cocktail party.

Things heated up with his coworker, he continued, and eventually, for reasons including but not limited to the existence of his emotional mistress, Sam and his wife separated. When I asked him what now, he told me that he was "figuring out his head." He'd started dating and sleeping with his colleague, emotions and all. She had a kid from a previous marriage and was, he said, bright and compatible with him in practically every way. In Sam's words, "It's hard for me to find somebody as smart as I am." That lucky girl must have been a genius.

So, Sam continued, he had feelings for his new girlfriend,

coupled with guilt about leaving his wife, and his new studio apartment was lonely. When he spoke of his coworker, his lust for her was apparent, but globs of superiority marked his description of who she was. He spoke of wanting to cook for her. He told me she ate "crappy, processed food" and that he wanted more than anything to make her an organic meal. Yeah. I mean, who did this woman think she was? How dare she cut corners to feed herself and her son by shopping at Stop & Shop instead of splurging at Dean and Deluca. He also told me that he didn't want to commit to her yet—now that he was single, he wanted to play the field a bit.

I warmed my hands over the campfire Sam kindled with his own self-regard, digesting the organic information he was nice enough to serve me. I told him that, in my opinion, his coworker had probably been waiting for him to leave his wife so, she assumed, he could be with her. That she'd been patient and probably wanted Sam be a father figure to her kid, but instead, she wound up graduating from an emotional affair to become another girl with soil worth tilling while Sam sowed wild oats.

He seemed flummoxed by my response and pulled the kind of maneuver they only teach you in Advanced Placement narcissism classes. He said he didn't understand why I wasn't sympathetic to his *wife?* Why did I care so much about the girl who eats junk food? I guess, I admitted, I felt bad for both, but related more to the girl who waited around.

I couldn't deal with Sam for much longer that night, and I haven't hung out with him since. I was turned off by his view of the world as some crazy mecca, waiting for him to cast off his marital shackles so he could partake in its cartoonish abundance. Didn't he know how tough it is to find people you like enough to actually date? How "playing the field," for every girl I know, means "going to bed early at least a couple of nights a month to make the loneliness stop screaming for the night" or "occasionally having to try making conversation with a man who's told you, unironically, how great he thinks Billy Joel's *Glass Houses* record is"?

I know there are guys who feel that marriage—to anyone— is a trap and unnatural. I know monogamy is wrong for some people, and certainly it's human nature—at least as a kid—to want as much as someone will let you get away with. But don't expect me to side with a bachelor soliciting sympathy for the burden of juggling women devoted to loving him. I will give that guy nothing.

I HEARD back from Leo after sending him my e-mail, and he was pretty relentless pursuing me the day after I cancelled lunch. He told me that his "situation" was "vague" lately. I wondered if his wife knew how "vague" he thought their "situation" was, because I'm pretty sure there's no less vague situation than being *married*, or, you know, *not*.

I resisted my lizard brain's attention to the "vague" quali- fier he tossed out like a rope from a height, and asked him, in spite of what I really wanted, to evaporate. As though he had been programmed to do the exact opposite, he sent me, in response, a promise that lunch would be platonic, two poems, a link to a photo gallery of the sea grotto he was going to that weekend, an MP3 of a Pretenders song, and an admission that he didn't know what a maxi dress was, then, a follow- up e-mail saying that he'd Googled, to find that a maxi was "precisely the kind of summer dress he found 'über-hot,'" adding, "Ouch."

"You want to have an ouch-off?" I replied, done with him. "You're married. I win."

And so it went. Leo went away. I was re-lonely. But the silence was brief and soon met with a chorus of "well done's" from friends who told me I did good, heading off at the pass a could've-been affair before it ruined my life, or at least the first half of my thirties. It was not easy to turn down the advances of a guy so out of touch with single-hood that he actually made romantic gestures, like sending poetry and coming right out and telling me how sexy I was, and other things I wasn't used to getting from men without wives.

And who knows if it would have even swelled to an actual affair if Leo and I had actually gotten together for lunch that day. I just knew that an hour and a half across a table from his fortyish good looks would've made me even hotter for him. And, like I said in the e-mail, I'm not in my twenties anymore. I don't want to seek out drama any more than I want to stub my own toe in the hopes it would make me a better artist, able to "feel more."

At that point, I just wanted to fall in love with somebody who was available and uncomplicated, so that things wouldn't be so hard anymore. And though I didn't know it was around the corner, I wanted to clear the table, in case the waiter came around with the kind of cake I could chew and masticate. I wanted to know then that, just like Big Edie, I'd, one day, have everything I wanted.

SECTION five

the house of no

"[P]eople with self-respect have the courage of their mistakes. They know the price of things."

—Joan Didion, *Slouching Towards Bethlehem*

"Remember, we dancing girls are honor bound to keep on dancing."

—Cynthia Heimel, *Sex Tips for Girls*

old acquaintances

've never been one of those people afraid of getting older. Maybe it's because I seem to get happier the further away I get from elementary school, and maybe it's because I've always had good adults around me, like my parents, who were examples of what older people can be like when they're not awful. Beyond the ability to teach you hilarious new words for sex, I don't see the romantic allure of youth. The baby-fat faces of those chimps on *NYC Prep*, the ersatz hip-hop posturing of white teenagers from the suburbs, the hairless bodies, the orthodontia, the awful clothing, the vampire shows: All of it is off-putting to me. But most of all, I'm not overly fond of young people because, with the exception of fictional characters Little Man Tate and Doogie Howser, they just aren't as smart as older people. They haven't lived long enough to know about stuff with cultural roots deeper than "Remember *Full*

House?" and most of them aren't too curious about learning what came before *them*.

I started feeling my own transition from young to smart, appropriately enough, on New Year's Eve—that of "Baby New Year" and "Old Man Old Year" iconography. It was the last day of the twenty-ninth year of my life, and I had a few different plans with girlfriends I was weighing for the night ahead. My friend Donna was going to a party in Williamsburg, which I was only beginning to hate, so I tagged along. She schlepped me to a loft party hosted by a model friend of hers. Model parties are the worst, because they have terrible snacks and beautiful people, and when you look at the beautiful people, they only make you want delicious snacks. Donna got bored there, so she ditched me to race to Times Square, yes seriously, so she could kiss her boyfriend by midnight in the Hell's Kitchen apartment she swore had an "awesome view of the ball drop," just like every TV in the country. I wandered the streets debating my next move, and then it was eleven thirty, so I hailed a cab to get to another party my friend Becky told me was at her friend's place, right near the Lorimer stop on the train.

I had a street address, but no cross street. The cab driver asked where to, so I had him drive straight on the block I had written down as I stared out the window at revelers in cocktail dresses, watching the street numbers slowly descend. We passed the BP gas station, and Broadway, and the other landmarks I recognized, until we were in a residential neighborhood far away from anything I'd ever seen before. The condos turned into projects, and the projects turned into tenement buildings, surrounded by leafless trees and carless streets. Orthodox Jews dwindled from groups to pairs, then there was the odd lone rabbinical student, and soon there were no more people on the sidewalk at all. My cabbie kept driving.

"How much further?" the driver asked.

I checked my phone: it was 11:50 p.m.

"I'm not sure. It's number seventy-six."

The numbers on the apartment buildings outside my window read 354 and 352. I tried calling Becky, but she didn't pick up or text back. Finally, we pulled up in front of number 76, a grubby walk-up. A girl in her early thirties with dyed green hair, a presumed reveler, stumbled past the front door. She looked methy and had no companion. As Green Meth got buzzed in, I realized from the safety of the backseat that this party spelled bad news. There was no way it couldn't *not* be fun. And I'd never be able to get home once I made what I'd hoped was going to be a quick appearance, which also seemed like a fat chance. I was miles from any train station, Becky had no car, there weren't any cabs that drove near this neighborhood unless dumb Jewish girls forced them to, and nobody in the city can get a car service to pick up the phone on New Year's Eve. If he dropped me off at 76 Whatever Street, on the corner of What The Fuck, I would be at that party indefinitely.

The cab driver pulled up to the curb and looked at me in the rear view mirror.

"Do you want to get out?" he asked me.

"No," I replied. "No, I don't."

I was relieved he gave me the opportunity to hear my thoughts spoken out loud.

Without wasting another minute in the middle of nowhere, the driver hit "reverse" and slammed on the gas, desperate to get back to a zone where drunks paid cabs for rides. The speedometer hit 60; he knew that he wouldn't hit any other cars if he drove backwards as fast as he could, into the abyss.

It was 11:55 p.m. when I realized that my decision to say no to that party had landed me face-first into the plot of a Sandra Bullock movie. *"Who will kiss me at the stroke of midnight?"* I panickedly wondered to myself as though it were important, behind a plastic console and a Moroccan immigrant driving backwards on the icy streets of the most deserted non-desert terrain of the country I'd ever greeted with bare eyes. I called my friend Michelle, who was at a roof party in the neighborhood, and she told me to stop by.

So I did, and I got to hug Michelle in time for the fireworks and the rest of the ballyhoo, and honestly, it was all perfectly fine. A relief, truly: the kind not worth its build-up. And I thought to myself, never again will I do something that dumb; will I buy into somebody else's notions of what has to happen on New Year's Eve or Valentine's Day or all the other stupid designs in place to time your feeling bad with the rest of the world's calendar. Since when have I been so lame that I cared about stuff like that? Only sad sacks and conformists need things like no kiss on New Year's Eve to remind them to feel lonely. They're as bad as the people who need St. Patty's Day as an excuse to get drunk or Halloween to wear slutty outfits. You can feel sorry for yourself and dress like a hooker all year round: Hallmark never needs to know.

I stretched my arms out on the roof at that party with Michelle and all her tattooed, skinny friends, sucking in the night air. I remember walking to the lip of the building to better see the skyline of sweet, wide Manhattan and thinking about how good it felt to exist in a negative space. To know what I was *not*.

How the kids around me, the ones who looked good scowling in photos, and got laid constantly and had access to phenomenal cocaine and implausibly flattering vintage clothing, could probably never write a story like I could, or be as good of a friend. How I knew there were people more easygoing than me; who would have said "What the heck!" getting out of that cab earlier, and would go sniff out the offerings of that party without a single worry about how they would get home later or how late they planned on staying.

But who knows whether the easygoing people in your life who can sleep with somebody and then move on, or take you to a party only to ditch you for Times Square, were going to be around in the long term. Would they be there if somebody you thought you could fall in love with disappeared without a trace and you wanted to talk at two a.m. about how much you missed him, or how secretly you think you're exactly like the person in your life you hate the most, or about how you're afraid of failing at being a writer?

I thought about how lucky I was to be different from how I was before. How I used to mistake "yes" for "yay!" and the pursuit of knowledge for the possession of it. I thought about how trivial people used to be better company to me than solitude, and how I'd finally earned the ability to shut out clutter—at least occasionally—and to leave self-sabotage to the kids who can't enjoy being alone now and then. The ones who do not believe deep down, even through the gauze of thick doubt, that they have what it takes to rise to the top, like cream. And I took relief that night in knowing that someone, somewhere else knew that too, and that he'd *get* me, once he finally got the chance to make my acquaintance.

★   ★   ★

"NO" IS a word that has different meanings, depending on your age. When you're a kid there's the apathetic "no," the cynical "no," the "no" you use because you don't want to try a gross-looking food or learn how to multiply fractions. Then, in your twenties, you try saying "yes," because you're racking up experiences. But eventually, you figure out that unless something seems outstanding and un-missable, it usually feels better to turn it down. And the name for that stage of life is "your thirties."

Michelangelo said that he makes a sculpture out of a marble block by removing everything it's not. Pretty smart stuff from a guy who made pizza pies in Boston! I'm thinking of the right Michelangelo, right? He has a chain restaurant? Wears a toga? Anyway, it's nice to know that once your twenties are over, you don't have a bunch of extra marble weighing down your silhouette.

You don't feel compelled to go out with guys who smell like bad news, and you don't have to do things you know will not be fun, like hauling your ass to a gig for some band you've never heard of so you can spend three hours on your feet, switching your purse from shoulder to shoulder.

Your twenties are the worst part of your life that you don't actually know at the time is terrible. Being a teenager sucks too, but you're aware of every last second of it. I decided to write this book right before I turned thirty, as a way to say good-bye to saying yes to things that don't make sense.

THERE'S A fantasy I've always entertained about connecting with somebody who hated as much about the world as me. Somebody cranky and contrarian, who loved dishing about successful people we both knew who sucked, but meanwhile liked my friends without any reservations. In my quest, I gave too much leeway to guys who seemed negative enough for the job, and they ended up hurting me. Alex, the critic, whose job it was to have a snide thing to say about every band you'd never heard of. Ben, who had nothing but self-deprecating insights into how lousy he was, without taking any responsibility toward what it was about him that made him insufferable. Jonathan, the man-child with the kid who wouldn't return a text unless it was at his own leisure. The more I heard "no" from them, the more I felt "yes"—that they were it. But the older I got, the more I liked about the world, and the better I got at figuring out what was game for tearing apart, and what was best to leave alone. It's the difference between cynicism and criticism; you need to be more of a grown-up to tell the difference.

The Critical No is the one you grow into. When you use it, it's to save yourself from future turmoil you reckon is beneath, or at least behind you. The biggest prides I've taken since graduating my twenties lay in the risks I took in turning things down. I said no to a dumb reality show after I read the contract, even though I had no other possibilities on the horizon at the time and was starving for cash. I quit smoking pot once I realized I did not need help being hungry. I got rid of the people I outgrew, and I fended off pests who tried to get back into my life.

Like, last week—I got a "friend request" on Facebook from this awful woman I went to college with. She was one of those friends I had that I didn't like, but kept around for company. She found me online and wrote me a little note saying "Long time no see! I'm up to the typical three B's: Book, Baby, and Brooklyn!" And I clicked "Block" so quickly that the rush felt like crack cocaine. I only wish I'd had the balls to click

"Report This User" so the FBI could've kept her on the potential sex offender list in time for her to start shopping for expensive preschools.

But I digress. Around this time of graduation or evolution or whatever you call becoming thirty, I started fending off the guys I didn't like *before* I slept with them. It was the first change I noticed in my behavior that really marked my twenties being over.

And. Thank. God.

OF THE multitude of characters I'm relieved to *not* be, I'm most grateful that I'm not one of those women who fights against time like somebody buried alive, scratching at the lid liner of her coffin. I cheerfully ushered in my thirties the year that began with a cab tour of What I am Not Land with the knowledge that I can confidently pass up opportunities that don't make sense because there'll be better ones on the horizon, even if I have to wait.

But I only know that kind of peace since I've given myself a break. All of a sudden, at some point, it became no longer necessary to punish myself for every transgression I made, like eating candy before noon or not writing a feature screenplay every week. Once I was rid of the chemicals in my brain that blocked out patience with anger, I could start making more informed choices about what makes me feel good and whom I allow to make me feel bad. In other words, I could start liking myself. And I began letting myself like people who have that in common with me.

I WROTE this book to make the people who read it feel good. I didn't write it to make anyone feel bad. I don't want to be

mean, and I've never been a bully; I was always the one bullies picked on. And the picked-on are the ones who are able
to be funniest when we *are* mean for that very reason: We've
had plenty of time to think of the best insults, being smart and
misanthropic and isolated all. So it's tempting.

And it was also tempting to wrap up this selective romantic
autobiography with a pat story about how I have a boyfriend
now.

Because as I write this, I've been involved with somebody
for a little less than a year—and it's *great*. He's a grown-up,
he's smart, he's kind—he's fantastic. And I could tell you more
about it, in all of the terms of an idyllic destination, but when
I was figuring out how to end this book, I had to think about
what it was I wanted to accomplish in the first place.

If it wasn't just notoriety and snark and serving the dish of
revenge all hot over dudes' laps, I figured that the only way I
could write it was if I thought the people who would read it
would somehow take some kind of solace in what I had to say.
That they would relate to the sad stuff that's funny if I did my
job right, and marvel at the stories they're grateful to experience only from the safe distance of a spectator.

And how on earth would my readers be able to take away a
positive message from the proceedings, and feel good, if they—
if you!—are single, and I'm not, and we've spent all this time
together, only for me to end the book with something like,
"Hey everybody, good news! Everything's fine now: *I'm* in a
relationship! The end!"

You'd hate me. *I'd* hate me! It would be dumb and false and
cheap and easy, and also, it's just not the point.

So, there it is.

This is not a book about me at all. And who am I to say

whether we can't be satisfied alone, or happy while we're looking, or whether the destination out-ends the means, or that it
was all worth it for the sake of meeting this guy. I wouldn't tell
you to do the same things I did, and I can't tell you whether
they would yield the same result. So, for that reason, it doesn't
matter if I have a boyfriend or not.

Besides, he won't let me write about him anyway.

acknowledgments

I want to start by thanking my valiant literary agent and occasional rabbi Scott Mendel, who appeared, *Brigadoon*-like, in the middle of a WGA strike to ride sidecar on my trek from writer to author. Thanks also to my fabulous, whip-smart, and golden-throated editor, Lauren Marino, and her wise, charming, and eternally patient assistant editor, Brianne Mulligan, for investing so much time and energy into a book with perhaps one more Oskar Schindler joke in it than you would have liked. Profuse thanks to everybody at Gotham Books, too, especially Bill Shinker, Lisa Johnson, Anne Kosmoski, Cara Bedick, Lisa Chun, Eileen Carey, and Ray Lundgren.

I want to thank the wise and supernaturally largehearted Holly Schlesinger, for guiding me through this project from its inception to its panic attack–laden completion, and for

Acknowledgments

absolutely everything else in between, except for the time she told me that Tootsie Rolls had trans fat in them.

Thanks to real-life rock stars Rachel Dratch, Patton Oswalt, David Rakoff, Jill Soloway, and Sarah Thyre for wading through sloppy early drafts and inspiring me by example.

Thank you Michael Rizzo, Dave Jargowsky, and Cooper Johnson at RZO Management, and Jaime Wolf and Angelo DiStefano at Pelosi Wolf Effron & Spates, LLP.

Thanks to Daniel Jones of *The New York Times* for publishing my *Modern Love* column, and to all those who wrote me after its publication to tell me how much they connected with it.

Thanks to the singular and fabulous Liz Phair, for generously allowing me to reprint her lyrics, and Phoebe Gellman, for being so ridiculously helpful in the process, not to mention for sending me the fifteenth-anniversary reissue CD of *Exile in Guyville*.

I want to thank my friend Nate Harris for the kind of enduring platonic love previously only known to me from the motion picture *Beaches*. Thanks also to John Haven, David Ozanich, Jesse Murray, and Joe Reid of *That's Important!* for being such important collaborators and fabulous friends.

Thanks to pals, mentors, colleagues, and occasional coconspirators Kent William Albin, Mike Albo, Tara Ariano, Scott Brown, Tyler Coates, Bart Coleman, Brendan Colthurst, Gabe Delahaye, Em and Lo, Renata Espinosa, Adam Felber, Susie Felber, Emily Gould, Anne Harris, Cynthia Heimel, Sarah Hepola, Ron Hogan, Sean Johnson and everyone at *Best Week Ever*, Diana Joseph, Colleen Kane, Erin Keating, Anthony King, Will Hines, and everybody at the Upright Citizens Brigade Theater, including the UCB Four: Amy, Ian, Besser, and Walsh, Michael Kupperman and Muire Dougherty, Molly Lambert,

Acknowledgments

Sarah Larson, Jeremy Laverdure, Jodi Lennon, Todd Levin, Therese Mahler, Chris Manzanedo, Emily McCombs, Michael Musto, Pauline O'Connor, Stephanie Pasicov, Dan Powell, Aaron Rothman, Gary Rudoren, Mike Sacks, Tom Scharpling, and Terre T., Rachel Shukert and Ben Abramowitz, Madeleine Smithberg, Caissie St. Onge, Arian Sultan, Paul F. Tompkins, Bruce Tracy, Conrad Ventur, and Jason Woliner.

Special thanks to Eryn Oberlander for her encouragement and insights.

Most of all, I want to thank my family for believing in my talent and showing me unheard-of amounts of unconditional love with a consistency that rivals the sun's rise and fall, and my boyfriend, Jack, who is absolutely the best man I have ever met in my life. He promised me from the moment I told him I was writing this book, three dates in, that everything would be okay. He was right.

About the Author

Author photo: © Conrad Ventur

Julie Klausner is a comedy writer and performer who has appeared in many shows at the Upright Citizen's Brigade Theatre, and on VH1's *Best Week Ever*, where she is currently a staff writer. She has written for *Saturday Night Live*'s "TV Funhouse" and *The Big Gay Sketch Show*, and her prose has appeared in *The New York Times*, *New York* magazine, McSweeney's, Salon, Videogum, and others. Her Web site, predictably, is www.julieklausner.com. She lives in New York City.